Encountering Christ

Robert Scott Stiner

Study Guide by Gail Hartranft and Robert Scott Stiner

Printed in the United States of America

Published by Pleasant Word, a division of WinePress Publishing, PO Box 428, Enumclaw, WA 98022.

ISBN 1-57921-548-3
Library of Congress Catalog Card Number: 2002116743

Dedicated to

Judy

&

Bill

Acknowledgments

With loving appreciation to:

Trish my wife and living proof
that Proverbs 31 is
not a myth.

To Eugene Hallum for teaching
Sunday school for over 50 years,
Thank you for giving to
The Lord.

Rodger Brant and Tom Corbett
(The thing about Godly men,
they are easy to spot, even
from a distance).

My editor Reagan Adee

Dr. Ed Glasscock for teaching me
how to teach Sunday school and
being the start of my own
restoration.

My friends at Moody Memorial
Church in Chicago, you
know who you are.

Contents

Foreword

Do you ever think that maybe we just have too much?

I first became acquainted with Robert Scott Stiner last year when he handed me a copy of his first book. As a result of my enthusiasm for that book he asked me to write the forward for this one.

I read Restoration while my wife Sandy and I were in West Virginia celebrating Thanksgiving. While there I picked up a copy of the local newspaper the "Exponent Telegram" of Clarksburg, West Virginia and read a very interesting column by the regional editor, Nora Edinger, entitled "Perhaps, just perhaps, Americans have too much to be thankful for."

She writes that "pecan pie looks unappealing when you've already eaten to excess . . ." And then observes

"Perhaps that's why many Americans seem to shoot straight from Halloween decorations to Yuletide ones, with only a brief pause to wallow in the best food of the year. We largely ignore Thanksgiving because we just can't get a grip on the whole gratitude thing."

Do we already have too much to the point that we aren't very grateful for what we have? Perhaps it's because, in a material sense we have no needs . . . everything we need we can get.

Why bother God with our needs when everything else is promised by MasterCard?

This book, however, seeks to change this attitude. It is about people—in the Bible—who in their most desperate moments reach out to Jesus.

Could it be that the simplicity of "just believing" escapes us in this world of plenty so that we're never quite in the position where we say "my son can be healed and this Jesus can do it." Or, "If I can just touch His clothes I will be healed."

Restoration caused me to reflect on my own healing. I was born with a brain hemorrhage—two of my siblings had already died of a similar brain hemorrhage—and I lived as the result of an all night prayer meeting because my parents had become Christians and summoned their local church to pray for me through the night. The doctor promised that I would either be a vegetable or I would die. But my mom believed that I could be healed and "Jesus could do it." He did.

No MasterCard or 21st century technology can meet those kinds of needs.

In our home when I grew up there was a plaque on the wall that read "With God All Things Are Possible" Matthew 19:26. Read this book and Robert will tell you that "When things are impossible, Christ creates possibilities."

So as you go through this book whether you're reading about the wedding at Cana, the nobleman's son, the healing of the paralytic, the adulteress woman, or Mary and Martha, you'll rediscover again about a Jesus who cares, who loves you, and who wishes to restore you to Himself.

Doug Ross, President
Evangelical Christian Publishers Assoc.

Introduction: From My Heart

I have sat in my office while writing this book and found myself amazed at the power of the written Word. The Bible stories examined in this book haven't changed. They are the same ancient stories with the same ancient people, and yet I had no clue to where the accountings of the lives of these people were taking me. It was like telling a story that you didn't know the ending to until you had arrived there. I guess it's because of the place in life I find myself at these days. It's not necessarily that I have become wiser now that I'm thirty-eight years of age as much as I have become older and less hardened—less hardened in my view of the disillusioned, and very much hardened at what televangelists, so-called healers, and the number-counters of Christianity have done to people. The way in which I see things now has shifted compared to ten years ago, or ten days ago, for that matter.

While researching these specific people who were in Christ's life during His three-year ministry, I have found that He didn't look *at* them but rather saw *through* them. He saw not what they were asking as much as what they were *really* asking, and that has made all the difference to me. When people cry out for help, they cry out to be helped at that moment. However, when Jesus answers and heals, He heals the present and the past as well, so that one can have hope for the future. He doesn't change only that moment in one's life, He changes everything.

Others that Christ came in contact with had great faith, brilliant statements, and what I call *humble boldness*. And He honors that in a person today in the same way He did in these accountings.

In writing each chapter, I have attempted to get inside each of the people, look at the world through their eyes, and see their culture as they saw it. In doing so, at whatever level I was able to accomplish it, I have found myself having to walk out of my office and take deep breaths just to get away from the pain that I brought upon myself in seeing what some of these men and women went through. I have cried like a baby as I have watched Christ see the truth in a sinner. He has the ability to take it all away and replace it with a love that defies any definition that English or Greek or any other language can try to confine. "Restoration," the title of this series, is an accurate description of the work of Jesus. When He came into contact with the men and women in these stories, He put back into their hearts and minds that which never should have been taken away. Does He not do that for us all?

So this book is a poem that can't be written. It is a love song that can't be sung. It can only be lived out in the hearts and lives of those who are willing to try. And the eternal faithfulness of Christ will prevail and be lived out by the men and women of this book.

But this book is not about hurting folks who have been restored by Jesus. It is about Jesus and how He restores hurting folks—and that is a big difference. I found myself wanting to step in constantly and stop what Satan or the Pharisees were attempting to do to the people; and Christ did. That is one of the reasons why He allowed me to write—and you to read—this book. My final point is this: Jesus restored all these people, and I know that no matter where you are in your life, if you reach out to Him He will do the same for you.

Robert Scott Stiner

CHAPTER 1

Two Daughters

Matt. 9:18–26; Mark 5:21–36; Luke 8:40–56

The hardest thing Jairus ever had to do was leave the side of his daughter, who was gasping for air. And yet, knowing he may never see her again, he leaves home, hoping that his final attempt will work.

When Jesus was around twenty years of age, a daughter was born into a family not too far away from where He lived. This was not just any family but that of a great man. His name was Jairus, and he was loved and well respected by the community, and that may be part of the reason why he was appointed as ruler of the synagogue.

Today we might call the position in our churches president of the board of elders.

Jairus was steeped in tradition. As ruler of the local synagogue, he knew and practiced all the religious intricacies according to the Law of Moses. In this type of profession, one can begin to live a life of circumscribed behavior and hidden feelings, which is demanded in rigid cultures such as this. Now his only child, a daughter, was, by the grace of God, born into the world, and his family had reason for a great celebration.

In another part of town, a young lady started her monthly cycle, which was as normal as the rising of the sun that brought the light of day to the small fishing community. Perhaps for her it was the time to walk through the open door of womanhood and take her place in the Jewish culture of having the honor of bringing life into the world for herself.

And all the while Jesus was in the carpenter's shop a few miles away, working to help support His family.

In those days, at the six-month point of a newborn's life, there was a good chance the child would be safe from the ailments that could cause an infant to get sick and possibly die because so little was known about medicine. The six months had now passed, and Jairus and his wife had another reason to thank God. God had shown favor upon them and given them the wonderful gift of blessing their newborn with good health.

For now, we will leave the little girl to come back to her later in the account.

Six months had passed and the other young lady was still bleeding. Now what was thought to be very normal had instead become very abnormal, and the flash of trivial news in this small village spread like wildfire. A barrier had been raised between the minds of the townspeople and the heart of the woman. The culture of the day believed that if this bleeding did not pass in the normal amount of time, then God was punishing you, and you became an outcast in the minds of the people. The woman was now panicked and began to wonder what she had done wrong that God would punish her in this way.

The Law of Moses is what the Jewish nation lived by and followed to the strictest letter. in Lev. 15:25–30, the Law says that a woman who continues bleeding in this way is unclean. This meant she had been spiritually defiled and was unfit to worship God until she became spiritually cleansed; however, she couldn't be until the bleeding had passed.

The passage in Leviticus also states that if a woman was unclean in this way, she couldn't sit on or touch anything, because if she did, it in turn would become unclean. Then if someone touched the unclean item, that person became unclean as well, at least for the rest of the day. So no person could touch the woman or anything she touched. And as if that weren't bad enough, an unclean woman couldn't enter the Temple until she was made clean again. Not entering the Temple meant not worshiping God, so her communication with God was cut off.

Still there was far more heartache placed on the young woman. In Mark 5:25–26 the evangelist mentions four specific problems the woman experienced:

1. She had been bleeding for twelve years.
2. She had endured much at the hands of many physicians.
3. She had spent all she had.
4. And she didn't get better but rather grew worse.

The six months turned into a year, the year turned into two years, and the chronic menstrual disorder never went away. It had lasted for twelve years as we catch up with her account in the scriptures.

The woman begins at some point to look at her options. The Jewish people of her day use the Law of Moses (known as the Torah) for instruction and teaching, but they also have the Jewish Talmud, which was created by men and used for instruction in civil and religious law. In the Talmud, there are eleven different remedies for this state of a woman, and I am convinced that at some point, when she realizes that her situation is not going away, she begins to try them. And as humiliating as they are, I'm sure she eventually tried them all. They were superstitions that somehow became legitimized by being written in the Talmud. Here are two of the extreme remedies listed in the Talmud: to carry around the ashes of an ostrich in a linen cloth in the summer or a cotton cloth in the winter; or to carry barleycorn that was found in the dung of a white female donkey.

Now these are ridiculous superstitions, as we now know, but they are some of the remedies for this condition found in the Talmud. And a person who has come to the end of her metaphorical rope will try anything. This woman feels guilt, but it is guilt born of man's superstition, not from anything she has done.

Enduring much at the hands of many physicians. That statement by Mark in verse 26 says many things to us, none of which are good. Did she suffer humiliation? Did she suffer abuse? How about physical pain? All we know for sure is that she endured much from many doctors.

And she *has spent all she had.* Along with all the other problems, the burden of financial poverty has been heaped on her as well.

Suffering at the hands of many physicians, bleeding continuously, and spending all the money she has, she finds herself not helped at all, but rather continuing to grow worse with each passing day.

This is a poor woman.
She is anemic.
She is sickly.
She is broke.

And she has been stripped of the three things that give a Jewish a woman her worth. The first is to bear children. She can't, because of her constant bleeding.

What Jewish man would want to marry a woman whom God has cursed by taking away her ability to have children? The second is her domestic responsibilities. She can't clean a home because anything she touches will be made unclean. She can't make a meal for anyone because the food will be made unclean, and no one can eat it without being made unclean. Third and worst of all, the woman has been cut off from entering the Temple. Worshiping God is part of the very fabric of the Jewish nation. To have this stripped from her is the most devastating blow of all.

This woman is a social outcast, made so by a rigid community that could not see past its own distorted views. If there has ever been a spiritual desert, this woman has collapsed in the middle of it. No one wants anything to do with her. The people believe that if God is against you, then who could be for you? Her misery creeps into my body and chills my bones even as I read the account.

After twelve years of living in this condition, I wonder if the woman has resolved that this is just how she has to be: alone. The steady thump of criticism can turn the strongest of wills. I wonder if she has no hope. She is a woman with nothing to live for. She is an outsider among neighbors and has become the poster child for what can happen to a person who disobeys God. She is as alone as it's possible to be. I wonder if this wounded woman is just waiting for despair to consume her small flicker of life until her death.

But wait!

Jesus is no longer in the carpenter's shop, for His public ministry has begun. And the woman finds out that this Jesus of Nazareth, the one who has performed miracles, is coming to shore. And somehow, with an ability that I don't think I'd possess if I were in her shoes, she has enough faith to try one last-ditch effort. She comes up with a plan: to get close enough to touch the tassel on His outer garment. She probably feels unworthy to speak to Him or get His attention. So she says to herself, "If I can just touch His clothes, I will be healed." It sounds perfectly normal in comparison to some of the other failed remedies she has tried.

She almost certainly disguises herself. It's likely she won't have the chance to plead her case if others recognize her before Jesus sees her. They all would cry "Tamei! Tamei!" (Unclean! Unclean!) Her chance for healing would be over before it began. Maybe she overhears the begging of Jairus, the very one who has barred her from entering the synagogue, and she doesn't want to stop Jesus' mission for the twelve-year-old girl? That's certainly possible.

The crowd is pressing in on Jesus as they always do. And as He makes His way toward the home of Jairus, the crowd follows very close, anticipating what He will do for their beloved synagogue ruler's daughter. With her head and face covered, the woman is able to press her way through the crowd. No doubt she touches many people in her attempt, thus rendering them "unclean." She makes her way through the crowd. She can now see

Him just ahead of her. She reaches out, and her hand grazes the tip of His garment. At that moment, something almost unexplainable happens. The warmth comes into her hand, into her arm and into her entire body. She freezes in the movement and feels the healing in her body instantly take place. She has just been set free from her suffering.

Jesus feels power go out from His body, and He stops. He turns around and, looking at the pressing crowd, asks, "Who just touched my clothes?" Taken aback by the question, the disciples answer, "What do you mean? Everybody is pressing in on you and touching you, and you ask, 'Who touched me?'" But Jesus is looking out at the crowd, only half listening to the answer given. As He continues to look, He says, "No, it was someone who deliberately touched me, for I felt healing power go out from me" (Luke 8:46 TLB).[1]

His disciples, the crowd, and Jairus all seem puzzled by the statement. Nevertheless, the woman knows. She is still close enough to Jesus to hear His question, and she knows that she is caught. She begins to shake in fear as she walks up and falls at His feet. On her knees, looking down at the ground in shame, she begins to tell the story of the past twelve years of her life. She speaks of the suffering at the hands of physicians, of being a social outcast, and of God being angry with her. In tears, she tells Him that she has no money left and has not been allowed to enter the synagogue for the past twelve years. She tells her ridiculous plan of disguising herself just to touch His clothes. And she tells Him that it worked, because when she touched His clothes, she felt in her body that she was instantly healed. And all the while, the crowd, Jairus, the disciples, and Jesus all listen to her testimony.

Now comes restoration.

When she has finished speaking, Jesus does something amazing. He does something that occurs only once in all of the scriptures when He speaks directly to a woman, and it is here that it takes place. He does not address the woman commonly by calling her "woman," as He did every other woman that He came in contact with. Instead, He calls her

Daughter.

For Jesus to call her "daughter" is much more than being respectful, it is a term of endearment. It is like saying, "You are a daughter of Israel and a child of God. And it is not God who has punished you, but it is God who heals you."

And for the one who has been treated as a social outcast, as if God found no favor in her, the Son of God completely changes everything. With one sovereign word, Jesus takes the woman with the lowest self-esteem imaginable and gives her more worth than she ever could have hoped for. He changes twelve years of thinking—not only her way of thinking, but that of all the townspeople as well. Jesus the Messiah, in front of everyone, places her in a position where He has never put any other woman. So her status in the community is raised above all other women because of His words. She is a daughter of God in spite of the past twelve years, in spite of what others believed about her and in spite of what she thought of herself. The imprint of Christ will be on her forever.

How do the townspeople feel about her now? The Messiah loves her, and now the people who once shunned her welcome her with open arms. Throughout history she has been a beautiful symbol of what God can do through a life that appears to be worthless. You see, mankind looks on the outside, but God looks at the heart.

I'm glad we are not given the name of the woman in the account. I believe that this woman represents, to a degree, every woman at some point in her life.

> *Daughter, your faith has made you well; go in peace and be healed of your affliction.*

Have you ever felt like this woman in some ways? Or maybe you do right now. Do you have a very serious situation that you are trying to deal with? Maybe it's something that didn't seem to be that big of a deal a few years ago, but it has hung around and festered and grown, and you feel you can't do anything about it. Suffering at the hands of others can mean many things for you. Are you alone? I'm not asking if you have people around you. Are you alone? Really alone? Because of the past few years, do you not fit the mold of what the average church-attendee should be like? Do you have almost no faith left to believe?

If you feel like the woman in this account, I want you to know this:

Jesus is passing through your town.

And with the smallest amount of faith that you can muster, He will answer you. He wants you to know that that is plenty. It is more than enough and all you need to get His attention. If you reach out to Christ right now through a little, seemingly insignificant prayer, no matter where He is going, He will stop and find you in the crowd. Even though He already knows your needs, tell Him so He can hear you say them. The savior of the world and the creator of the heavens and earth calls you His daughter. That small amount of faith that took everything you had to believe in Him—He says that is what heals you. The belief in Him.

It must have taken some amount of time for the conversation between the woman and Jesus to transpire—no one knows exactly how long.

> But while Jesus was still speaking to her some men came from the house of Jairus and said to him, "Your daughter is dead, why bother the teacher any more?" (Mark 5:35)

Jesus ignored what the men had said as fear gripped the heart of Jairus. There must have been something about the brown eyes of Jesus[2] when you actually looked into them, because when he said to Jairus, "Just believe," he did.

The Journey

After Jesus finished the statement, they all started toward the home of Jairus. This journey, be it short or long, must have sent Jairus's mind reeling. What did he think of during that trip to his house? Of course he thought about his daughter. But what had Jesus just told Jairus to do ? *Just believe.* It's true that Jairus had enough faith for Jesus to heal his daughter. That's why he sought Him out. But to raise his daughter from the dead—well, that's another story. Where would he find enough strength to have the faith for something like that? What proof did he have that Jesus could do something of this magnitude? Could it be in what he had just experienced ? Jairus witnessed the woman—whom he and his people would not allow to enter the synagogue for twelve years because she was unclean—come up to Jesus and be healed because of her faith. And the same woman that Jairus called unclean, Jesus called daughter. Wow.

It is clear that these two accounts are not two accounts at all, but rather one and the same. Without witnessing what Christ did with the woman with the issue of blood, Jairus might not have heeded the words of Christ, but rather heeded the words of the men who said it was too late because his daughter was dead. So, it is very probable that Jesus allowed Jairus to see the faith of the woman in order to give him the faith needed to believe for his now-dead daughter.

If Jesus didn't stop and have the conversation with the woman, the miracle would still have transpired, but Jairus wouldn't have known about it until later, when she was pronounced clean. The woman's faith had ramifications far beyond what even she could have imagined. She affected the faith of one of the most well-respected men in the community—another proof that *all things work together for good for those called according to His purpose.*

So these passages in the gospels of Matthew, Mark, and Luke are about two main daughters. They're not about Jairus or the disciples. They're about two women: One is the anemic woman, whose faith in Jesus Christ touched everyone and everything around her.

What about Jairus' daughter?

Oh, that's right! I said this account is about two women. The other woman might be you. That's right, *you.* How much does God love you? Enough to put in His Holy Word the account of this woman, which wouldn't be there unless He wanted it to change your life. He wants you to get to know the person of Jesus, the compassion of Jesus, the love of Jesus. He tells you that you have worth—and not just worth, but extreme value. It is your faith—even if it seems almost nonexistent—that Jesus wants to explode into beams of light, in the same way that heat lightning cuts across the sky. And the same way that clouds move up in the west, splitting the sun into rays that spray in several directions onto the Midwestern farmland—that's what He wants to do with your life and shine His love to your world.

CHAPTER 2

The Wedding at Cana

John 2:1–11

Six days have passed, and everything about the wedding is a success. With fresh new guests arriving each day from the various towns and villages of the region, the director of ceremonies is happy that all is well and yet still as busy as a hummingbird on a spring day.

The guests are greeted outside, then brought into room where they can relax from their travel and have a foot bath prior to entering the dining room. The celebration of food and wine is enjoyed by all; still the responsibility of the director is vast, to say the least. He has someone in charge of lighting the dining room. Candles are placed in several areas, and lanterns hang from the ceiling, shining on the beautiful banquet table. There are the foot washers, the cooks, and the headwaiter; sleeping accommodations for everyone; and a fresh supply of wine, with provisions for the proper wine to be supplied at the proper time. There is the registration of guests—and don't forget the bride and groom, without whom there would be no celebration. It is a lot to keep track of from early morning until late into the night for seven relentless days. Still, everyone enjoys a time of festivity and merriment when everything works as planned.

Mary hears some commotion in one of the side rooms where the food is being prepared. Being part of the wedding staff herself, she goes to investigate. She spots the director of ceremonies and some of the servants frantically trying to find out what has happened to the wine. A gross miscalculation is the only answer anyone can come up with. "How could this have happened?" one says to another. "Were there more guests than anticipated?"

"Not really. We thought there would be more who showed up than registered, but still we had plenty of wine."

"Well, we do not have plenty of wine now, and this wedding is about to be ruined. The remainder of the guests will go without wine. What are we going to do? No one will ever hire me again as wedding director—not to mention that the bride and groom are going to be humiliated, and the guests who are not here yet will have nothing to drink."

As Mary overhears this, she tries to think of a solution.

Five men are lagging behind a little and talking among themselves:

"Why would Jesus bid us 'Come follow me' and then tell us we are going to a wedding of a friend of his?"

"What does a wedding have to do with us?"

"All we need is to have Jesus teach us the truths of God. Nonetheless, if he said we are going to a wedding, then we'll go with him to a wedding."

As Jesus and the disciples near the home, they are greeted and the appropriate introductions are made. It's possible that the shortage of wine is due to the five whom Jesus has brought along, but only five extra people shouldn't be a problem. Still, there's no way of knowing. The significance is that the wine has run out.

When the wine ran out, the mother of Jesus said to him, "They have no wine."

Mary comes to Jesus with a sense of urgency in her voice and lets her son know that something needs to be done.

Mary knows the angel Gabriel came from heaven thirty years ago and announced to her that she would conceive a child from the Holy Spirit and that His name was to be Jesus. She also remembers the circumstances surrounding His mysterious birth: the wise men, the shepherds, the expensive gifts, and the dreams. How could she forget the dreams her husband had, causing him to move the family for the safety of her son? She's known who her son is from the beginning, and for her the biggest confirmation came when she found her boy in the Temple, completely baffling the wisest of men who had come to listen to the child's wisdom and knowledge. Like no one else, Mary knows her Son and she knows He will do what is right. Even when she does not quite understand His methods at first, she still believes in Him—

- because of their thirty years together;
- because of raising him from an infant to manhood;
- because of the angel Gabriel's announcement;
- because of the shepherds and wise men; and
- because of the Temple experience.

She has seen it all, and because of his unwavering consistency, she has learned the lesson that many of us still struggle with: No matter what the situation, He has the answer.

What a lesson is in His first miracle. What a life-changing experience we will all go through if we can grasp and hold on with all our might to this truth.

We see a need. We bring it to Jesus, even if it is not our own. Even when we do not quite understand His methods at first, we believe that He will do what is right. Like Mary, however, we learn His unwavering consistency through time and experience with Him.

Back to the passage at hand. Jesus responds to his mother and says:

Woman, what does that have to do with us? My hour has not yet come.

At first glance, this statement seems a bit cold and distant, but that would be from our cultural perspective; let's look at it from His. "Ma'am, we just got here; what shall we do? It's not time for my ministry to start." Now if He had said this, we could understand it quite a bit better—right? Well, that is exactly what he did say, only in the terminology of his day.

After the statement by Jesus to his mother, she gives instructions to the servants:

Whatever He says to you, do it.

Does this not speak volumes to us about the faith Mary has in her son, and about the eighteen years of His life of which we have no record in the scriptures? "Even though this problem is potentially disastrous, my son has the answer. He can fix this, and even though I don't know what He is about to do, do whatever He says."

She simply does not hesitate to step out on a limb and share her faith in her son, because for her it is not stepping out on a limb at all. Her faith in Him has been building for years. The more time we spend with Jesus, the easier it is to totally trust Him. Now someone's need is brought to the King of all Kings, and, because of Mary's faith, the creator of the heavens and the earth begins His first miracle as a man.

There are six stone water pots of at least twenty gallons, each used for washing hands before and after eating at this celebration, and Jesus says to the servants to fill them with water. The servants not only fill them, but they fill them so full that they're about to run over. Nothing else can be added.

- Then Jesus takes the ordinary and makes it extraordinary.
- He takes the plain and makes what no one could explain.
- He takes the average and makes it exceptional.
- He takes what no one wants and makes it what everyone wants.

Jesus instructs the servants: "Draw some out now and take it to the headwaiter."

No doubt the servants have quite a conversation from the time they leave Jesus and the water pots until the time they reach the headwaiter. As far as they know, they are bringing him a cup full of water. I imagine the conversation going something like this:

"The headwaiter is standing over there; go and give him this water."

"I am not giving him the water; you give it to him. Look how upset he is; he needs wine for the guests, not water."

"You know we are about to be yelled at, do you not?"

"I know we are, but what choice do we have? This is what we were told to do."

The servants go up to the headwaiter and hand him the cup, then take two steps back. He takes a sip. First, a puzzled look crosses his face, and the servants think, *We are about to get it now.* Then the headwaiter starts to smile. His smile breaks into laughter, and now the puzzled look is on the servants' faces. As the headwaiter's sorrow turns to laughter, he says, "I think the bridegroom has kept this from me until now," and he rushes off to find him.

"What just happened here?" says one of the servants.

"I have no idea," replies the other.

The headwaiter thinks the bridegroom is responsible, but the servants know that whatever has happened to the water, the bridegroom had nothing to do with it. Jesus, Mary's son, did whatever happened.

The headwaiter speaks to the bridegroom and finds out he had nothing to do with this extremely fine tasting wine. Now let's just think about this for a minute. This is the end of the text; however, I am sure it is not the end of the story. I am sure the bridegroom and the headwaiter both want to find out where the wine came from, so they track down the servants and ask where they got it.

"We gave you water, sir; we are sure that we gave you water."

"Taste this for yourselves; this is not water. Who told you to bring this to me? Show me where this wine is."

The servants now taste an extraordinary wine. Then, still puzzled, they take the bridegroom and the headwaiter to the six stone water pots, and they all see and taste some from each of the containers. There are one hundred and twenty gallons of the best wine they have ever tasted. The servants' eyes are widened and their hearts jump with elation as they recount exactly what they were told to do.

"Jesus, Mary's son, told us to fill these purification pots with water, so we filled each of them to the brim. Then He said to draw some and take it to you, and that is it, but we know it was water. Jesus changed it, but we did not see anything happen."

As the wedding party hears this, I'm sure they are stunned and in awe at what Jesus has done. Mouths drop open, a buzz starts around the guests, and his disciples are amazed, as is everyone present. I'm sure Jesus is now the center of attention.

Some no doubt have heard what happened a couple of months ago at the Jordan River with Jesus and John the Baptist, so the conversation now is all about Jesus and who He is.

Personally, I would love to know more about what happened after the water was changed into wine. We know that John knew, because he was there, but he made all the spiritual points necessary in the passages he wrote for us.

In this first of Jesus' recorded miracles, there are at least two lessons he gives us to draw strength from and to help us today in this very hour.

1. A need was brought to Jesus, and He responded. He always responds. He responded in a far greater way than anyone could have imagined. He took a seemingly hopeless and disastrous situation that was brought to Him and transformed it to show His glory, and everyone around reaped the benefits.

   Just like the wedding, something in your life—or maybe your life itself—is on the verge of becoming a disaster. Because of it, as with the wedding, some will become angry, some will go without what they need, and some will be disgraced. Bring this problem directly to Jesus. Tell Him what is about to happen. Maybe you caused it, and then again, like Mary, maybe you had nothing to do with it. You do not have to know how He will handle it; just believe He will do what is right, and then watch. Jesus will use the situation to get all eyes on Himself. He has done it in my life, and I know He can do it in yours.
2. Jesus has the power to take the ordinary, the plain, the simple, and transform it into something to manifest His glory.

   Are you a housewife? How about an assistant to a pharmacist or a grandparent? Do you feel like just another number in corporate America? Did you grow up on a farm? Did you grow up around Indiana? Do you look at your life as ordinary, plain, or simple? The water was transformed into the Lord's best, and, let me assure you, that is exactly

> what He wants to do with you, no matter what you think of your life.

Where you have come from is not important to your Savior when compared to where you are heading. However, it is important enough to die for. He will transform you, and those around you will reap the benefit of what He alone has made.

Our life is not the water or the wine in this story. We are the container, the stone water pot, the vessel, the carrier.

We are empty because of our empty lives, and we don't realize there is nothing in us until someone is directed to share God's love with us. When a servant of the Lord obeys—does what he is directed to do—and shares the gospel with someone who does not know Jesus, He fills that person to the brim. The servants have done what they were commanded and told another about Christ; thus he is full. However—

To know about Jesus is water, but to know Jesus is wine.

Once we hear the word of God, we have the potential to be changed. Once we understand, we are full. Once we believe, Jesus transforms us.

Water is to wine what knowledge is to belief. Now when we believe that Jesus is who He says He is, the water of our hearing His word is instantly transformed to the wine of us believing His word. Salvation has occurred; thus our lives have been transformed, restored.

When the people at the wedding drank of the wine that Jesus had miraculously given to them, it caused all who were around to worship Him. When the people around you taste of the wine that Jesus has miraculously given to you, exactly the same results will occur. It will cause all eyes to focus on Jesus. It will start a buzz, and those around will see Jesus in a totally different way. And because He has done this countless times in people's lives, including my own, I know he can do it in yours.

CHAPTER 3

The Nobleman's Son

John 4:46–54

A Lesson on Prayer

A man tries to concentrate on his work, but his thoughts drift in and out like the tide lapping against a tired seashore. His son has an illness, and the last of the physicians of his land has just informed him that there is nothing that can help the boy now. With this response, the tide of his thoughts washes out to sea, along with the last of his hopes that his son would grow to be a man, have a family, and live a long and fulfilling life. Being a powerful man in Capernaum means nothing when you can't even save your own son, and the phrase "wealth cannot buy health" rings all too clear to this nobleman on this sad day.

With a bang, the door to the nobleman's office swings wide open. A messenger enters the room with exciting news. The nobleman lifts his head only slightly, but not even enough to see the servant, and says nothing. The servant, almost shouting, says, "A thousand pardons, Master, but I have come to know that Jesus of Nazareth is no longer in Judea."

"What is that to me?"

"Sir, about a year ago this Jesus was the one we all heard of who changed the water into wine at a wedding in Cana. Over a hundred people testified to this." The nobleman's eyes are now fixed on the servant, as he himself remembers hearing about the Cana wedding.

The servant continues speaking. "And Jesus, at this last Passover, was in Jerusalem and performed many miracles, and large crowds are following him and his teachings. People are coming to Him with all kinds of health problems, and He is healing all who come and ask."

A thousand thoughts race through the nobleman's mind all at once, but the one at the forefront is *My son can be healed, and this Jesus can do it.*

There is a huge mass of people over by the market in the dusty little town of Cana, and as we look in for ourselves, we see Jesus in the center of the group. The crowd itself has three types of people in it. There are the ones who believe He is who He says He is and are willing to follow Him wherever He goes. The disciples, as well as some of the people Jesus healed, are part of this group. Secondly, we see the people who know Him by their association with other people, or maybe they grew up in the same area as he did. Now that He is a miracle worker with new teachings, He is being taken very seriously, and so many are saying all these wonderful things about Him, these people are there to lay claim to what is rightfully theirs. As they see Him in a new light, they want everybody to know he is their friend. Finally, the rest who are crowding in on Him are the ones who just came to see the miracles. They don't care one way or another who He says He is, this is fascinating stuff and it's like nothing they have ever seen before. This is the greatest type of amusement and they want to be a part of it.

Jesus is fully aware of who is around him and what their intentions are. Still, like a hundred times before, He chooses to teach them the truths of the Kingdom of God. As the teacher is in mid-sentence, a man starts yelling from the outskirts of the crowd.

As he pushes his way to Jesus, asking for pardons along the way, Jesus stops the teaching and waits as the man approaches. He finally gets to Jesus, but his labored breathing causes him to take a moment before he can speak. He gathers his composure and begins. He says, "Sir, I am a nobleman from Capernaum, and I have traveled this distance because I need your help. I am a powerful man in my region, but I am helpless in the matter for which I have come. I ask this of you as a father. I have a son whom I love dearly and he is very sick. When I left him to find you, he was at the point of death. Please come with me back to Capernaum and heal my son."

As the crowd hears the nobleman's plea, they all lean in to see what Jesus is going to do. Jesus leans back and, knowing the hearts of the people, addresses the crowd first.

He says:

Unless you people see signs and wonders, you simply will not believe. (John 4:48)

The nobleman says to Jesus, "Sir, come down before my son dies."

Jesus has compassion on the father of the dying son and says to him:

Go; your son lives. (John 4:50a)

And for the first time in recorded scripture, Jesus heals someone without being there.

The crowd didn't see anything happen, but the miracle still took place at that very moment. I'm sure the miracle watchers felt cheated. "Hey, we came to see some miracles, and if you keep doing this, we might as well go home. This is not any fun for us." And the ones who wanted to say, "See that? I know him; we grew up together," had nothing to say at this time as well. However, there is a fourth type of person added to the crowd at this moment. It's the nobleman.

The narrative says:

> *The man believed the word that Jesus spoke to him and started off. (John 4:50b)*

Although he did not see anything, he totally believed what Jesus said, and that was good enough for him.

The confirmation of the nobleman's son's healing came on the journey back to his house. His servants told him what happened, and the nobleman was able to ascertain that his son was healed when Jesus spoke the words.

CHAPTER 4

The Pool Bethesda

John 5:1–14

Learning to Walk Again

Have you ever been trapped in sin? No, that's not what I mean, I mean really trapped in sin. Trapped for so long you have lost all hope. You've stopped trying. You don't care. You've given up. You remember the spiritual mountaintops that you enjoyed climbing once, but now you find yourself in a valley, cultivating the easy fields of whatever it is that has you trapped.

Have you resolved that even though you can see the way out and the steps to take, you can't do it alone?

Oh, people have come by with good intentions, but their assistance would fall far short of what you really need. Time seemingly has a way of proving and sealing what we think to be true. Less and less hope becomes hopelessness, and hopelessness, when it is full grown, becomes despair. And although despair is never comforting, it can become familiar and you can get used to it. If you have not experienced what I am talking about, at least on some level, skip the rest of this chapter, because this is for those who have been there or who are trapped by this heaviness even now.

OK, follow me on a little trip, and I'll take you to the answer. I know the way because I've already been there.

Come with me back in time about twenty centuries ago, when sin could do what you think it has done to you now.

Here we are in the first century, and this ancient city we stand looking at is none other than Jerusalem. On this bright, clear morning, as we stand on this hill, we see all her beauty. These are the shorter days of autumn, at the time of the Jewish holiday feasts, and a sense of joy and anticipation in the air reminds us of our childhood a few days before Christmas. In the city, there are humble homes and happy children, and from where we are, we see the busy workshops with hardworking men and marketplaces with fresh vegetables on the northern suburbs of the bustling community. There is a road that travels eastward and disappears over the Mount of Olives through Bethany to Jericho. Off in another direction, there are a handful of sheep grazing in a field, and their shepherd is resting under a shade tree.

We can travel anywhere in Palestine, and this is the type of city we will find. However, there are a few things that make this city a little different, and one of the differences is why we're here.

The Sheep Gate, as it's known, is back behind us; the sheep market is near the gate; and down the hill, beside the sheep market, is our reason for coming. As we walk down the hill, we see the "Pool Bethesda," as it's known by the people who live in the region. It's a small water pool, made from a natural underground spring, surrounded by five porches that consist of a floor, some columns, and a roof. And as we get closer, we see a pitiful sight: scores of people fill the porches and the area all around the water. Some are old, some are not so old, but they all have something in common: they have something wrong with them. We see the sick, and we see the crippled. Some are having seizurelike symptoms; others are blind, and it becomes sadly clear that this is some type of gathering place for the ones not blessed with good health. There are a few who have come to give food, and others who have come to assist their friends or relatives into the warm water, but there are far more sick than there are those to help.

Today, if you wanted to find Jesus, you might first think of looking in the Temple; however, you wouldn't find Him there.

See the man walking up the road? See the ordinary man who isn't carrying anything? That's Jesus, the Messiah.

Jesus is walking to the Pool Bethesda. His eyes are fixed on a certain man. Jesus walks through the mass of hurting humanity to a specific man who is lying on a pallet for a bed; we also walk up and listen in. Jesus already knows the man is paralyzed and has suffered for thirty-eight years. As a matter of fact, He knows everything about the man. As He bends down with His eyes focused on the man, He asks him:

> "Do you wish to get well?"
>
> The sick man answered Him, "Sir, I have no man to put me into the pool when the water is stirred up, but while I am coming, another steps down before me."
>
> There was a belief at that time that an angel of the Lord went down at certain seasons into the pool and stirred up the water; whoever then first, after the stirring up of the water, stepped in was made well from whatever disease with which he was afflicted.[3]
>
> Jesus said to him, "Get up; pick up your pallet and walk." Immediately the man became well, and picked up his pallet and began to walk. Now it was the Sabbath on that day. So the Jews were saying to him who was accursed, "It is the Sabbath, and it is not permissible for you to carry your pallet." But he answered them, "He who made me well was the one who said to me, 'Pick up your pallet and walk.'"
>
> *Later that same day Jesus found him in the Temple and said to him, "Behold you have become well; do not sin anymore so that nothing worse may befall you."*

There is a clear indication here that the man's paralysis was due to some type of sin. And whatever the sin was, it had trapped him for thirty-eight years.

Somewhere in this span of time, someone came along with news of the Pool Bethesda. Someone told this man about the pool and helped him to get there.

But when he realized that he couldn't make it to the water first without help, his hope gave way to hopelessness. He could see the pool; he knew how to get there; but he couldn't take the steps alone. He thought he needed someone, anyone, to help him into the pool for his healing. But the truth is, he was looking for his healing in the wrong place, and he didn't even know it.

Jesus didn't come to the paralyzed man to help him to what he thought was the answer. Jesus came to the man to show him that He is the answer.

This is where my story ends and yours begins.

Sin traps us.

It's our sin that traps us. And although we do it to ourselves, we cannot correct it by ourselves. We need help. Sin paralyzes and causes us to be unable to stand spiritually, let alone walk. It can and does hold us captive. And because we see what has seemingly worked for others, we put our hope and trust in their advice.

It seems right.

It has some spiritual emphasis to it.

And all our time and energy and lives are being spent pursuing an answer that may not be there at all.

Then Jesus, the King of Kings and the Lord of all, spots *you* in that mass of hurting humanity.

He knows how long you have been there.

He knows the state you're in.

He knows you can't walk.

As a matter of fact, He knows everything about you.

He personally designed your DNA.

He, who sketched out what your fingerprints would look like, walks over to *you,* and as He bends down with His eyes fixed on you, He asks, "Do you wish to get well?" The obvious answer is yes, but that's not what you offer as your response. You give the means by which you are trying to get an answer. You say, "Sir, these are the books I have read, and these are the people I have spoken to and I can see where I need to be, but I can't get there without someone to help me . . . " Jesus stops you in mid-sentence and gently and simply says, "Look at me; listen to me. Get up; pick up your pallet and walk."

And immediately you will feel the strength return and you will become well.

Jesus alone has done it. Not Jesus and something, not Jesus and someone; Jesus alone.

And if you'll notice, He's not carrying anything, but He has brought something.

What He has to show you are scars—the scars on His hands and feet and side. These scars represent a price paid—not part of a price but a complete price. Jesus paid it all for you, and that's why you can stand again.

The pallet He commands you to pick up may be the bed of shame, doubt, and regret. But because of what Jesus has done, your wounds are not wounds any more, they're only scars. And without those scars, you can't identify with someone who has those wounds. That's why Jesus says, "That which you used to lie on for support, pick it up and carry it with you as a testimony of what I have done for you and what I can do for others."

As you walk and go on, people will say, "Isn't that the one who was paralyzed by sin? What happened?" And there lies the seed for their healing!

CHAPTER 5

After the Storm

Luke 5:1–11

A Lesson in Following

The Sea of Galilee is truly a beautiful sight to behold. There's a rabbinic saying that the Lord "has created seven seas, but the Sea of Galilee is His delight." It's shaped like a harp that has been laid on its side. Its deep blue water is offset with barren rugged hills rising above 2,600 feet abruptly over the water on its eastern and western shores. It's very tranquil and peaceful to look upon, and the shoreline has all sorts of colorful wildflowers around different parts of it. The surface of the water is 685 feet below sea level, and this combination of high hills and low water makes its climate almost subtropical. Oh, and one more thing: this climate also makes it susceptible to abrupt weather changes and severe storms.

Zebedee has seen plenty of fishing nights like the one that has just passed, with that dangerous storm and its whipping wind and pelting rain. And he has even seen this much damage to the fishing nets from the mud and rocks that the storm stirred up from the sea bottom. But fishing all night and catching nothing is new, even to this longtime veteran of the sea.

And now, a minute or so before dawn, we hear the busy sounds of many fishermen up and down the seashore, cleaning and mending their nets. We can also see the silhouettes of Zebedee and four others with him because of their small campfire, and as the early autumn morning begins to brighten, we see something else.

Just down from the five men, a crowd is gathering and getting larger by the minute. Jesus is in the center of the crowd, which is getting out of hand, pressing in on Him and jockeying for position to listen to His teaching. The crowd has grown so large so fast that he can't possibly address them all. So He makes His way over to the five fishermen. Jesus gets into His friend Simon Peter's boat and asks him to row out a little so He can better teach the people.

Jesus begins to teach. Peter is beside Jesus as He teaches, not in the synagogue to a congregation, but rather on the Sea of Galilee in the open air to the crowd. And while Peter's boat serves as the pulpit, the people are amazed at the power that is in the truths of God's word.

For the first time they see what they always hoped was there:

God's word alive.

So Jesus feeds the people today with the living bread of God's living word. And when He has finished, the crowd begins to disperse with a new and more accurate perspective of their Creator. As they go their way, Peter, with a few strokes of the oars, gets himself and Jesus back to shore.

Jesus has finished teaching the crowd, but His teaching isn't finished. He will now teach another one. His message is for Simon, and the topic is what Simon knows best: fishing! Jesus now uses what Simon knows best to illustrate His point and show him in the clearest of ways what He wants of him:

> *When He had finished speaking, He said to Simon, "Put out into the deep water and let down your nets for a catch." Simon answered and said, "Master, we worked hard all night and caught nothing, but because of Your instruction, I will let down the nets."*

Simon knows the time for catching fish is in the night and the place to catch fish is in the shallows of the lake. The circumstances are wrong, but be that as it may, Simon will try again because Jesus said to. So he loads all the gear back into the boat and rows out into the deep. Simon doesn't let down the nets because the circumstances are favorable; he does it because Jesus said to.

After Simon and his partner row out in the deep area of the lake and let down the nets, something strange starts happening. They feel a tug on the nets that quickly turns into strong jerks. You know, the kind you get when you're fishing with a pole and you know you have caught a huge fish before you can even pull it in.

And these fish are strong enough to pull the boat around, so Simon signals for help from his partners to bring the other boat. Even so, there are so many fish, they almost capsize both boats.

And after the wild excitement of getting all the fish in the boats—

After everybody is completely soaked—

After the laughter and fun of trying to keep the big, flopping fish in the boats while rowing to the shore—

After thinking about what the catch is worth—

Simon realizes what just happened. He realizes what Jesus has done. And the realization turns into amazement at who this man is. Simon Peter falls down at Jesus' feet and says:

> *"Go away from me, for I am a sinful man, O Lord!" . . . And Jesus said to Simon, "Do not fear; from now on you will be catching men."*

So Simon Peter, his brother Andrew, James, and John leave everything and follow Jesus.

Jesus saw the storm on the Sea of Galilee the night before. He saw the men on the sea struggling all night, and when dawn had broken, He knew they had nothing to show for their discouraging labor. Actually, He allowed the storm, and He kept the fish away to show them the calling on their lives.

God will teach us in ways that we can understand, and He allows circumstances to develop in our lives in the same way He did for Peter.

You see, these four men already knew Jesus. They had already seen Him perform miracles.

They had already heard Him speak some of the powerful truths of God's word.

But now, He spoke to them directly to show them the very purpose of their lives. Now he said to them, through a lesson that a fisherman would completely understand, "Come follow me; from now on you will put out the net of God's grace into the deep waters of the world, and you will bring a catch of souls into the Kingdom of God." (My interpretation.)

If you do what Jesus commands, the catch will be so great that you will need to call for help to move souls from the net of God's grace into the boat of their identity in Him. The excitement of this catch can bring you much joy as you begin to realize the value of what He has done through your obedience.

Sometimes there are storms in our lives that we are sure we will not survive. They are long, and it takes all we have inside of us to endure. And when the night is finally over and dawn is breaking, you start to see the aftermath of the storm, and you have nothing to show for it but ripped and torn emotions. Many times this is preparation that God allows to happen because we think we are rulers of our own lives. We are allowed to experience things in our lives to get us to the point of understanding the message that God wants us to see. And when the turn of events takes place, and we know by the circumstances that it was the Lord who did it, we see the total picture of what He has done. It once again shows us our awesome God, and we find ourselves before Him on our knees, just like Simon Peter, broken and saying, "Depart from me, oh Lord; I am full of sin."

You've already known Him to a degree.

You've seen Him do miracles.

You've heard and seen the powerful truths of God, but now He is speaking directly to you.

And His message is the same for you as it was for Simon Peter:

Do not fear.

What you are going through or have just gone through was allowed by Jesus. And He says, "It was allowed so you can see that I am in the midst of it all. And your personal experience is so you can see who I am."

The clearer we see Christ, the more accurate our perspective is on reality.

The clearer we see Christ, the more we will catch souls for the Kingdom of God.

The clearer we see Christ, the more we understand the purpose for our trials.

CHAPTER 6

Delivering a Synagogue Demoniac

Luke 4:31–37

Restoration

It's the Sabbath morning, and Jesus goes into the synagogue at Capernaum to teach. He has with Him the four ex-fishermen of fish and current fishermen of men. Now the warm-hearted Galileans love to give themselves to the power of Jesus' teachings, and the frequency of His teaching cannot lessen the lasting impression He will make on their lives. As the scrolls are handed to Jesus, He unrolls them and begins to read from the word of God. The congregation sits silently as they struggle to understand the old language that Jesus reads. After finishing, He hands back the scroll and begins teaching.

Perhaps He teaches in the same way he did in the Sermon on the Mount: "You have heard it said this way, *but this is how I say it is . . .* "

The people are riveted to their seats. They hang on to every word Jesus speaks as He allows them to see God's words in a new light. They say, "He speaks with His own authority and power, and not like the scribes who merely speak the words of other scribes from the past." Jesus' teaching always has this underlying message: *The Kingdom of God is at hand. Repent! The Kingdom of God is before you at this very moment.*

Just as the people are unaccustomed to being told to repent, they're also unaccustomed to this type of teaching; they give complete attention to Jesus' new and refreshing style.

Then from within the synagogue came a horrifying shriek from a man possessed with an evil spirit.

The man with the unclean spirit glares at Jesus and cries out, *"What business do we have with each other, Jesus of Nazareth? Have You come to destroy us? I know who You are, the Holy One of God!" (Luke 4:34).*

The air is seared open as if with an evil knife, and immediately Jesus responds:

> *And Jesus rebuked him, saying, "Be quiet and come out of him!" Throwing him into convulsions, the unclean spirit cried out with a loud voice and came out of him. (Luke 4:35)*

After a moment, the man picks himself up and quietly sits down as ordinarily as any other person.

The people in the synagogue are seized with amazement. They cannot believe their eyes. They all know that exorcism of evil spirits is a lengthy process with a specific ritual. But at a simple word from Jesus, the demon submits to Him and leaves the man.

> Immediately the news about Him spread everywhere into all the surrounding district of Galilee. (Luke 4:37)

(Remember this verse, because in a couple of chapters from now I'm going to refer to it for a very specific reason.)

Jesus encounters a man controlled by an evil spirit, and when the confrontation takes place, Jesus, with a word, sends that demon packing.

Now there is no disputing that this story takes us to a world far from our normal way of thinking. Yet in the world we live in now, where mental sickness and neuroses are growing at an out-of-control rate, this account of Jesus doesn't seem too far from us at all.

The world that Jesus came into was truly a demon-haunted world, and it is very important to know that Jesus did heal the man. And the world we have today is no different, except that the enemy is far more shrewd than he used to be.

The fact that Jesus did heal demon possession is of immeasurable hope and meaning to us today. People today are haunted by demons of a different color. Today we can label them as follows: greed, worry, fear, insecurity, self-concern, and on and on.

The demons today do the same thing they did in Jesus' time: they take complete control of a person. Oh, they may not throw anyone on the ground, per se, but they will cause someone to crush another person on the way up the corporate ladder, or make someone feel insecure in comparison with a more educated or better-looking person.

See, there are many demons out there that still control people. The demon of loneliness, the demon of depression, and the demon of worthlessness are extremely controlling. And if you are being controlled by one of these, or one or more of a thousand different ones, then read carefully what I am now telling you.

The man in the synagogue somehow got to where Jesus was. I don't know if someone brought him or if he got there on his own, but the point is that he got to where Jesus was. The demon might have had power over the man, but it was powerless in the presence of the Holy One of God, Jesus. Jesus stopped teaching the people and saw a man being tormented by this demon. He cast it out, restored the man's soul, and renewed a right spirit within him.

You are standing before Jesus right now. You don't have to go anywhere to find Him.

And Jesus gladly leans in to hear you pray to Him.

You have His undivided attention. Tell Him what you think you need. He already knows what you do need, and when you cry out for help, He will respond. He always responds. What held you captive before will bow and submit to His authority, and you will be free. Jesus will restore you because that's the business Jesus is in:

Restoration!

CHAPTER 7

The Mother of Peter's Wife

Matt.8:14–15; Mark 1:29–31; Luke 4:38–39

On this Sabbath day, we are in Capernaum in a synagogue. We have just witnessed Christ's teaching and an astonishing miracle that He performed. He silenced, then exorcised a violent demon from a man in the congregation. Now, as the service comes to a close, we have a clearer understanding of God's love, and we have witnessed the amazing authority of Christ. It is mid-morning as we leave the synagogue. Although the Jewish law requires people leaving the synagogue to walk away from the building slowly as a sign of remorse, this crowd is reeling with excitement and wonder about what they have just witnessed. The people have been given a new way of seeing

God, and this brings a new sense of urgency because Jesus is in their town.

We follow James, John, Andrew, and Jesus, along with Peter, back to Peter's home. Peter's wife has stayed home from the synagogue because her mother isn't feeling well, and Jesus is going to be the honored guest of the family. It is amazing how much of Christ's life revolves around this little fishing community. Each time Christ visits, He has a reserved room waiting for Him at Peter's. It will soon become Jesus' second home because of the amount of time he spends there.

In the Jewish home, most of the work of preparing the Sabbath meal is accomplished the day before, so as to minimize the amount of work done on the Sabbath itself. As we arrive at Peter's door and go inside, we notice that nothing is prepared for the meal, as is the custom of the day. Instead Peter is greeted by his wife. She takes him aside. Panicked and visibly upset, she explains to him that her mother's burning fever has gotten worse and her mother is lying down in another room. (In these days, once a fever reaches a certain point, the patient almost never recovers.)

Jesus, notified at once of the woman's condition, immediately goes into the room. Her fevered face and helpless eyes turn toward Jesus. The bedding is damp from perspiration, and yet she shivers as if she is caught in a winter storm without a coat. She has broken out into a heavy sweat, and her temperature is far above what a common fever would be. All who enter the room have seen these out-of-control symptoms before. They know the fever will lead to delirium and then the inevitable if it can't be controlled immediately.

Jesus recognizes something about her condition that no one else is able to see. The fever is not a fever in the common sense of the word, but it is demonic. Jesus walks over, takes Peter's mother-in-law by the hand, and rebukes the fever, perhaps with the exact words he used to rebuke the demon-possessed man in the synagogue earlier in the morning. The fever comes out of her. She is now visibly calm, and the normal color has returned to her face. Jesus has instantly cured her, and now He helps His friend up to her feet. When the fever leaves, the cure is so complete that not even a remnant of her captivity can be found.

After she is healed, she walks straightway out of the room and finishes the preparations for the Sabbath meal. And what a meal it is as they all sit down to partake of that which is given them on this day. Peter and his wife are given back the health of a beloved family member. And the mother of Peter's wife is given back her gift of health and ability to serve. Just minutes ago, everyone was thinking of the worst possible scenario. But Jesus, with a word, changed everything.

The fever had Peter's mother-in-law prostrate in bed, but in the more medically developed countries, we don't really fear this type of ailment any more. However, we have a type of fever that is much worse than the one that affects the body. We now have the fever that affects the spirit and soul of mankind.

Today we can look at this miracle for guidance, because we, like Peter's mother-in-law, are the restless sufferer.

At first glance, one must wonder why this account was canonized. Why is this seemingly smallest of miracles, as compared to all the others in the scriptures, even brought to light? Without any stretch at all, it seems logical to believe that Christ performed far greater miracles than this that were never recorded. Why a fever? And if, as it appears, the fever was caused by a demon, it didn't throw her to the ground and shrill as so many did when He cast them out and sent them on their way.

I believe this miracle is recorded for several reasons.

One is that Christ is the only one who could have healed the woman. The instantaneous healing would leave no doubt in the minds of those who witnessed or experienced it. And a life that seemed to be at its end was restored at the touch and by the word of Christ.

When God sees fit, He allows us to experience events in our lives that are far more than just unpleasant. Early on in these situations, if He were to step in and rectify the problem, it might be easy to give the credit to something other than God. But once you reach a point in life where the only way out is if God steps in—then, when He does, the answer becomes crystal clear. I can't tell you how many times I have prayed, "O God, I have made a mess of things this time and I can't fix it," and the amazing thing is that they always get fixed. So the next time you find yourself in a frightening situation with a loved one, remember this account. And remember that when Christ is petitioned, He responds. He responded for Peter and his wife, and He will respond for you.

Another reason this miracle by Christ is recorded is to show that what is taught and displayed in the church is to be taken from there and lived out in the home. If this day in the life of Christ is taken as a whole, then we see Him in the morning teaching the love of God and displaying the power of God. He recognized a great need and met that need. However, if this power and love for another remain only in the church, they have no value. Let me say that again. The power and love of God that we learn and experience in the church service are worthless if they are not taken into the home. Our failure to understand this is one of the largest weapons for the opponents of true Christianity. Therefore, God in His infinite wisdom recorded this entire Sabbath day in the life of Christ for us to learn about.[4]

Another reason for this story is that Christ, when petitioned, responds. Let me clearly say that I am not speaking of petitioning Christ to give you more or expand your boundaries or anything along those dangerous lines. We have enough; we don't need more. This is a petition out of love and on behalf of another—what Martin Luther called "the gospel in miniature."

Another reason is that what might seem insignificant to some may be quite significant to those experiencing it—thus it is significant to Christ. At first glance, this miracle seems like a little thing to someone standing on the outside and looking in at it. But it was important to Peter and his family, much as a thorn in the paw of a lion is very important to the lion.

This is also the first *Diaconate* of a woman. She was healed by the touch and the power of Christ and immediately went into service for the Messiah, which really stands in the way of those who believe that there must be, in every case, a time of preparation before entering into a ministry of service to God.

Please don't think that you are any less important just because you don't stand in front of a congregation and teach from the word of God or haven't gone to seminary. That is what the worldly side of Christianity thinks, not your Creator. A person who serves a meal to someone who can't afford to buy one is the same as that seminary graduate who stands up and dazzles you with the word of God on Sunday mornings, in Christ's way of looking at it.

> *The King will answer and say to them, "Truly I say to you, to the extent that you have done it to one of these brothers of Mine, even the least of them, you did it to Me." (Matthew 25:40)*

This account also shows us the touch of the Master's hand. When Christ touches your life, you are made whole.

There is something almost unexplainable about touch. It's reassuring, it's comforting, and it causes a sense of identifying with the one who is touching you. But when Christ touches you, it's so much more. It's completing; it's beginning a work and finishing you wholly. In a way, He touched the woman, but in a greater way, He touched the spirits of all who were present by healing her. The story has continuously touched countless lives for a couple of millennia and it has touched me today.

That same evening, after a wonderful Sabbath meal, all who were in Peter's home were reflecting on what Jesus had done, first to the demoniac in the synagogue and then to Peter's mother-in-law. They heard some commotion in the street, so they all went to the window. There was a crowd getting larger by the minute outside Peter's home, and people were calling for Jesus to come outside and help them. So Jesus and His four disciples walked out of the house, and as they got close enough to see the people, they saw the ailing, the afflicted, and the crippled.

The people who were in the synagogue saw the power that Jesus had over the demon, and after the service had finished, they went straight to anyone and everyone who had any type of ailment and brought them to the street in front of Peter's home. The five men stood and looked at the ever-growing crowd for a moment as they all cried out for healing. It was about to turn into a mob scene because everyone was trying to get as close to Jesus as possible. He quickly calmed the crowd—to a degree—by making it clear that He would stay and heal everyone who needed healing for as long as it took. The compassion of Jesus went out to the people, and He began to heal, one by one.

CHAPTER 8

Healing the Paralytic

Mark 2:3–12

The Faith of Others

Jesus is at the home of Peter once again, and in this dry and thirsty land, even the rumor of His return can spark the wildfire of a massive crowd. These are days of excitement in Capernaum, and a new teaching with new power is at hand. Peter's little home is quickly packed with as many people as it can hold, and we feel the push and surge of the crowd as even more try to pile into the doorway to get close enough to hear Jesus. The scribes have a place inside where they continually evaluate Jesus' words and actions, and the disciples are trying to keep some semblance of organization.

Outside we see four men who have just set down their paralyzed friend, whom they have been carrying on a pallet. Their plan is to bring him to Jesus so that He can heal him of his paralysis, but they quickly realize that there is no way they can even get near Jesus because of the density of the crowd. Then one of them comes up with another way to get to Christ, and so they discuss their plan.

Back inside the house, a few minutes later, we see Jesus teaching the truths of God to the eager, attentive crowd who will soon forget the watchful eyes of the scribes. In the middle of the teaching, a distraction begins above Jesus on the roof and quickly becomes so dominating that He stops and looks up. Now picture with me the breathless surprise of the crowd as an opening in the roof begins to appear.

After it is made large enough, a pallet is slowly let down before Jesus and the crowd. Busy hands work to steady it and bring it safely to the ground. On the pallet lies a paralyzed man, his fevered face and hopeless eyes turned toward Jesus.

It is surely a marvelous sight, even at the time and under the circumstances where the marvelous might be an everyday occurrence. These men's energy and determination far exceed any that have been seen before. This open outburst of faith shines as bright as the sunlight in contrast with the dark clouds of unbelief within the hearts of the scribes. They have come for only one purpose: to watch, listen, and ensnare Jesus. But now the air is filled with silence and expectancy.

The men are still on the roof, looking down through the opening, and Jesus' heart leaps as He looks up at them:

And seeing their faith, he said to the paralyzed man, "Be of good cheer, your sins are forgiven."

Their faith atones for any lack of faith on the part of the sick man. Now we see that if faith is lacking in an individual, the unrelenting faith of others may still avail and bring the healing of Christ.

Jesus reads the scribes at a glance. They're angry that He would claim to forgive this man's sins and thus make Himself equal with God. So Jesus confronts the scribes and asks a question that they do not, or will not, answer. The room is filled with tension and silence. He then says:

"But so you may know that the Son of Man has authority on earth to forgive sins"—He said to the paralytic, "I say to you, get up, pick up your pallet and go home."

As the healed man slowly rises and silently rolls up his pallet, a way is made for him through the crowd. Astonished eyes follow him as amazement and fear fall on the crowd, and in His presence they glorify God.

CHAPTER 9

Healing the Shriveled Hand

Luke 6:6–10

Jesus said, "Get up and come forward" . . . "Stretch out your hand."

How many withered hands are there in the church today? How many people are not able to give a spiritual hand to their brothers and sisters, because they believe God can't use them as a result of something that has happened? Many people see themselves in this shadow.

If this is you, I want you to see something with me.

People who have been broken on the wheels of living are the ones whom God, more often than not, chooses to use.

Think about this example: Who can most identify with a couple who have just gone through a miscarriage? Answer: a couple who have already gone through it before. God graciously allows some to experience such sorrow in order to help others in that same situation.

Many times we experience a trial or hardship, and we feel that it overwhelms us to the point of not being able to do anything again in the body of Christ.

It is not our wounds that give us our identity.

It is the scars. The scars that Christ has healed make us unique and special. Scars are reminders of wounds that are now healed.

We must come to our own individual realization of what Christ has done for us before we can be freed of the unbelief that God can't use us.

If you have a withered hand because of something you have done or because of what was done to you, listen to these words. These words are a pool of healing for everyone who is willing to jump in.

Christ is no longer speaking to a man in a synagogue, but He is still speaking. And now He is speaking to you!

He says, *"Get up and come forward . . . Stretch out your hand."*

And by doing so, you are holding out in front of you that which keeps you from laying hold of the tools of God.

If you notice, you are already healed.

CHAPTER 10

The Centurion's Servant

Luke 7:1–10

Have you ever felt unworthy to approach God in prayer? Have you ever thought God would punish you for a sin in your life, so you broke off all communication with Him? You stopped reading your Bible, praying, going to church, or trying in any way? Or how about this: have you ever felt that you're not worthy of the kind of love God has for you, because all you have done is to choose to sin in the face of that love?

If you haven't, then I am thankful that a spiritual remnant are still living. However, you are an endangered species. For the rest of us, who stumble and fumble our way through this precious life and have felt more than a little inadequate for God to visit us, we have a gift: We can identify with some very special people in the word of God who can open our eyes to His compassion in a different way.

The people of Capernaum look out of their homes into the deep blue Sea of Galilee, with all its beauty and tranquility. It is the source of life for all. In parallel, throngs of these same people have looked to Christ, with His compassion and grace, as He provides a sea of healing for body and soul.

After the Sermon on the Mount, Christ returns here to His temporary home to rest. But, as always, many who heard His words are following him.

While He is there, a party approaches Christ that is no ordinary party. It is made up of Jewish elders who, by definition, are some of the most trustworthy men in all the land. They come asking Christ on behalf of a centurion to heal his gravely ill servant. Now if there were ever a man worthy of something from Christ, it is the man they represented.

Jesus and the crowd that has followed Him listen as the elders earnestly implore Him, saying, "He is worthy for you to grant this to him, for he loves our nation. It was he who built our synagogue. He loves his servant to the point of sending us to ask you to come and heal him."

Upon hearing this, Jesus starts for the centurion's home, followed by the Jewish elders and the crowd. As they approach the home, the centurion is notified that Christ is near, and he sends another party of his friends out to meet Him. When his friends reach Christ, they repeat the exact words of the centurion: "*Lord, do not trouble yourself further, for I am not worthy for you to come under my roof*" He goes on to say that he understands authority, and that he believes Christ can heal his servant without being there. After Christ marvels at the centurion's faith, He heals the servant.

The elders told Jesus the centurion was worthy.

The centurion told Jesus, "I am not worthy to even approach you," but he still believed.

Jesus didn't just turn to the crowd and say that the centurion had faith. He said he had *great* faith.

One of the most marvelous points of this account is this: realizing we are not worthy is the first step in being worthy in the eyes of God.

Understand that what you do for God does not make you worthy of anything.

CHAPTER 11

The Widow at Nain

Luke 7:11–15

The heat of the day has passed, and the white sun has turned to a big red circle. It lies behind a thin cloud cover, and we are cooled by the long shadows because of its setting. We find ourselves standing by a dirt path on the outskirts of a small village called Nain. We see hawks riding the early evening updrafts off in the distance.

Looking in the direction of the village, we see coming toward us a great procession, the characteristics of which are unmistakable. We see a funeral coming at us as we hear the well-known blast of the horn, which carries the tidings that once more the Angel of Death has taken someone. It started from the home of the departed, made its way through the village, and now is out past the village walls coming towards us. The air is being filled with loud lamentations, flutes, and the melancholy tinkle of cymbals. The dead body is that of a young man. We see that he has died fatherless, for only a woman walks in front of the open casket, called a bier. His body has already been washed and anointed. He is wrapped in the best the widow could procure; significantly, these accouterments are known as "provisions for the journey." In passionate grief, the mother has torn her upper garment as they make the slow, methodical walk to her son's final resting place. There in the earth, she will render his last sad office and, with a burst of terrible sorrow, say her final farewell.

But in all this painful pageantry, there is nothing for the heart of this poor widow except the desolate thoughts connected with the Jewish mindset about being childless.

As the funeral procession makes its way out of the city, we see red dust floating in the air. In the other direction, coming toward us up the path that leads to Endore and Galilee, streams another great multitude. Their leader is the Prince of Life. Here on the path before us, life and death are about to meet. The question is, which of the two will give way to the other?

From a distance, Jesus recognizes her as she walks before the bier. She is still weeping, even after He hastens a few steps in advance of His followers toward her. She has never seen Him before.

Now the connecting link between them is the widow's deep sorrow. This Jewish mother has touched the heart of the son of Mary. Those bitter, broken tears, which blind her eyes so that she can't see who stands before her, are the strongest language to Him. He feels compassion for her, and in the presence of her grief, death will not continue.

Jesus walks from her to her son. As Christ touches the bier, those who are bearing it stand still. The greatest of all defilement is that of touching the dead, but it means nothing to Christ. At this moment, none who are watching can anticipate what will follow. At this moment, death bows and gives way to life. One sovereign command, and he who was dead sits up and begins to speak. The men carrying the bier instantly set it down and back away in fear. But Jesus takes the son and gives him as a gift back to his mother.

God sees your tears. He sees your struggle to hold it together as you face the inevitable. It may be that the events of your life are already set in motion, and you find yourself living out the procession. There is the death of a loved one, and there is the death of a relationship, which brings its own brand of potent grieving. We grieve, and rightfully so, at many things in our lives. The loss of a home or a job, the loss of our innocence in a thousand ways, or the loss of something of sentimental value—they all cause different types of pain. Grief is a powerful emotion and normally must run its course. But Christ has a way of giving us the most unexpected of gifts in the midst of our pain.

Troubles are real in this life. They are inevitable and they can be relentless; I am not denying this fact. All I want is for you to always look at them through the eyes of the previous paragraph. Keep what God has done in its proper perspective, in relation to the pain and troubles of this life.

When things are impossible, Christ creates possibilities. This same God paid a ransom for you. It is paid completely, without any doubt or controversy, and that payment changed you forever. You were dead and waiting for your body to catch up and die too. Then you believed that Jesus is who He says He is. At that moment, death bowed and gave way to life, never to reverse again.

CHAPTER 12

The Adulterous Woman

John 8:1–11

It is early morning, and the dawn of a new day is breaking in Jerusalem. The disciples have each gone to their own homes, and Jesus has decided to spend some time alone. He has been staying with friends in Bethany and spending time in the grove on the Mount of Olives that He is so fond of. He spends His time there in prayer and communication with God. This day, Jesus has already made the two-mile walk into the city and is in the courtyard of the Temple. The early light begins to illuminate the scene for us. The people have all gathered in anticipation to hear His teachings for the day, and so we listen in as well.

In another part of town, a couple is in bed, fast asleep—not a married couple, but a couple of adulterers. They are hidden from the world until they are startled awake. The door is kicked open and the covers are yanked from the bed. The woman screams, and the scribes yell, "Adulterers, adulterers!" The man and woman break out into an instant sweat as they are exposed and shamed. It appears that the man is allowed to grab his things and slip out, for these so-called protectors of the law have what they came for: the woman.

"Get up, put this robe on; come with us!" The woman is pushed out of the house and into the streets as she thinks to herself, "This can't be happening, it has to be a nightmare."

The scribes and Pharisees tell her to start walking toward the Temple and say nothing else to her. She begs, "What are you going to do?" But there is no response from the men, other than evil stares. As she is pushed through the streets, the whole town watches. Tears and sweat from her face run together, and she clenches her jaw and tightly presses her lips together. She knows it is only her they were after and not her lover, but she can do or say nothing in her defense.

Back inside the Temple, as we listen to Christ illuminating God's love, a commotion is coming down the street and into the courtyard. It's a lynch mob of the religious leaders of the day, forcing their way through the crowd. They disrupt the teaching and get in front of Christ. They push the woman forward, and she stands before Jesus.

The Pharisees said to Christ:

> *Teacher, this woman has been caught in adultery, in the very act. Now the Law of Moses commands us to stone such a woman; what then do You say?*

The woman knows she is captured, and she now understands why she was brought to the Temple. She hangs her head, and her long, disheveled black hair hides her face—but nothing can hide her guilt and shame. The One she has been placed before is her judge. There is no escape, nowhere to hide, and she knows it. She realizes her fate; she is dizzy and about to faint as she waits, standing alone. It all hangs on His verdict, and yet He gives no response except to stoop down and write in the sand with His finger.

Even the lightest of thinkers present have figured out that this is a trap for Jesus. The religious leaders continue to press Jesus for an answer. The woman slowly raises her head, because the One asked to judge her says nothing. The intensity in the air is almost tangible. The religious leaders sense a feeling of triumph: they have trapped this self-proclaimed Messiah. They think any answer He gives will be wrong. If He says nothing at all, He will, in effect, be agreeing she should be stoned to death. And if He declares that she should not be stoned, then He will be accused of teaching against the laws of Moses. The religious leaders have ensnared Jesus, and they were able to do it with an insignificant, adulterous woman whom they have used as a pawn. However, no woman is or will ever be insignificant to Christ.

We want Jesus to give these heartless scribes and Pharisees their deserved reward for humiliating the woman. We all lean in and wait to see what He will do. His heart is turned toward the woman, and He does not give an answer, but rather gives *the answer.*

Jesus slowly rises up and levels His eyes with the accusers, looking at the oldest—the ones who think they are the wisest—and says:

> *He who is without sin among you, let him be the first to throw a stone at her.*

His answer is controlled and metered, yet it contains the most profound of truths. And this simple answer stuns everyone. It is so far removed from anything the scribes and Pharisees have thought or felt. No one in the lynch mob wants to even pick up a stone, because in doing so, they will be professing to God that they have no sin. No one moves—except for the angels in heaven as songs of praise erupt in a thunderous roar for the Savior of the world, and the heavens shake. Satan watches a mirrored portrayal of judgment day unfolding. (Although we don't hear that part when it happens, it certainly does.)

Then Christ looks back down at what He was writing in the sand, as if to be finished with the mockery of the woman. He stoops back down and continues writing in the sand. The oldest men are the first to walk away silently. With years come understanding. The younger ones have more pride than wisdom, but not long afterward, they too leave.

Now comes restoration.

As we watch from the side, we see the adulterous woman standing alone, and a few steps in front of her is Jesus, still writing in the sand. Jesus glances back up and notices that she is still standing there. She has no idea what to do. I wonder what she is thinking. "Do I run away? Do I walk away? Do I thank Him?" What she does is just stand there and say nothing. But now Jesus stands up again and levels His eyes with hers; now will come her judgment. Jesus says, in almost a whisper,

> *"Woman, where are they? Did no one condemn you?"*
> *She said, "No one, Lord."*
> *"Neither do I! From now on, sin no more."*

Judgment day has come, and instead of receiving what she expects, she is pardoned. Jesus stands up on her behalf and says, "Forgiven!" And the One who has the right to pick up a stone never considers it.

I don't know what you are going through, and even if you could tell me, I'm not sure that I would fully understand. But I know One who does. It may be that you have been used, mistreated, or abused socially, mentally, or physically. I believe that the worst type of abuse comes at the hands of the so-called religious leaders of the day. You might even be partly to blame for the situation you find yourself in and know what you deserve because of it. Nevertheless, let me assure you that the heart of Christ is turned toward you. You have His attention. He has leveled His eyes with yours, and He says, "I have died and risen again so that I might proclaim to you that *you* are forgiven. *You* are restored. Don't sin any more."

CHAPTER 13

The Syrophoenician Woman

Matt.15:21–28, Mark 7:24–30

As she walks, she wonders what she will say. She goes over possible scenarios in her head: "What if He says this? How will I respond?" Over and over she practices as she makes the journey. She feels that only one opportunity will be given her, if any at all, but she is determined for the sake of her daughter.

A mother's love is a powerful force when put to a test, and this woman needs healing for her daughter. She is willing to pursue the slightest possibility of a cure. Even though this miracle worker is a Jew, this Syrophoenician-Greek woman has heard that He can cast out demons.

As her daughter lies in bed, tortured by an evil spirit, she leaves her side to cross a geographical line—as well as a religious line—to seek healing for her child.

Jesus and His disciples have left the crowds and traveled north, near the border of Tyre, for rest. They enter a friend's house so as not to be noticed, but somehow, as always, word gets out.

The woman finds the home and begins to cry out: "Have mercy on me, Lord, Son of David; my daughter is cruelly demon-possessed."

However, there is no response from Jesus. The petition of the woman grows louder and more persistent; she will not leave until she has gained an audience with Him. The disciples become annoyed by the constant begging of the woman. They ask Christ to send her away, and still the woman continues, "Son of David, have mercy on me!

The woman doesn't know how to address Christ. Her words are an appeal to an Israelite miracle worker, not to the Messiah. David has never reigned over her or her people, and yet she cries out to the Son of David. Jesus responds to her and says:

I was sent only to the lost sheep of the house of Israel.

Christ speaks these words, not to deny her petition, but rather to guide her in the path and teach her who He is. Now she doesn't know what to say. She breaks down, falls at His feet crying, and simply says, "Lord, help me!"

To grant the woman's request as she has stated it would not fulfill the reasons Christ performs miracles: to prove Himself to be the Messiah that he claims to be. It would reduce Him to just the miracle worker she thinks He is. Still Jesus cannot, will not turn His back on a person in need. He has every intention of healing her daughter, but not until she understands who He is. Anything contrary to this would go against the person of Christ as seen consistently throughout scripture. Therefore, He first teaches her in a manner and with terminology that she can understand for His purpose. He says to her:

> *Let the children be satisfied first, for it is not good to take the children's bread and throw it to the dogs. (Mark 7:27)*

In language for us to understand, He is saying to her, "The message that I bring must first be fed to the children of Israel before it can be fed to the rest of the nations of the world." (Nothing harsh is said here to this woman, as so many have taught, but rather, Christ speaks to her in a terminology she can understand.)[5] The proof of her understanding is in her amazing and perfect answer:

> *But she answered and said to Him, "Yes, Lord, but even the dogs[6] under the table feed on the children's crumbs." (Mark 7:28)*

Now she understands what Christ is saying to her, and in her response, she points out that even though they might not sit at the table with the children of Israel right now, the heathen—or "house dogs"—are still in the house. The dogs are still property of the master of the house, and the excess from the children's feast is more than enough to feed them. Being a daughter of Abraham puts her in the house of the master.

With few words but perfect teaching, Jesus causes her to see accurately who He is. Once she understands, He tells her she has great faith. And because of her answer, when she returns home, she will find her daughter free from the demon.

May the hearts and minds of countless people, Jews and non-Jews alike, be set free because of the teaching of Christ through the understanding of this woman. The depths of guilt, from heritage and alienation alike, melt away as scraps fall from the table. They must fall from the table so that we may partake in understanding who Jesus is.

Whether you choose to follow Christ or not, you are never outside His reach. If you call out to Him, "Help me, Lord!" He will respond; He always responds. He will restore you to what He wanted for you and your life all along.

CHAPTER 14

Jesus and the Samaritan Woman

John 4:4–42

It's early summer, and the sun is already a hammer at midday. It beats down relentlessly. The time of day is twelve o'clock in the afternoon, and it is hot. It's the kind of dry heat that parches your throat and causes dust to stir as we walk these dusty paths of Palestine.

Today we visit one of the Samaritan towns. Its name is Sychar, and it has much to teach us. We will wait here, a mile or so outside of the town, for our encounter.

First, let us look at our surroundings. Beside us is an old well. It stands near all these forks in the road where the ancient Roman roads meet and part, going their separate ways. However, this is not just any well—this is the well of Jacob. He dug it several hundred years ago, and it still stands as a memorial marker of the symbolic possession of the land of Israel. The road to the north leads into Sychar, and another climbs eight hundred feet and leads to Mt. Gerazim, with the Samaritan temple on it.

At this time in history, a well is a perfect place for the women of the towns to spend a few minutes together and socialize. In the cool of the morning or before the sunset, the women go to draw water from one of the town wells for the day's supply. In doing so, they inevitably meet other women from the community and have a moment or two to chat about the normal things of life. But not at this well—it is outside of town.

So here we are at this dusty fork in the road. From the direction of Judea, we see a small band of travelers approaching. Their unhurried walking causes the caravan dust to rise in the air around them. As they come into focus, we notice it is Jesus and His disciples. They have been walking for hours, and they are hungry and tired. As they arrive at the well of Jacob, Jesus tells the disciples to go on into town and buy some food as He decides to stay and rest. He sits down and leans up against the shaded side of the well, the disciples go to get the provisions. Jesus begins to relax.

As the disciples walk into town, a woman is walking out of town, toward us. She has austere beauty as she carries a water vessel balanced on her head. We notice two strange things. First, the time: it is the zenith of the day. Why would she be filling her water jar at the worst possible time? It is stifling hot—why has she chosen to get water now? Second, the location: there is at least one other well in the middle of town. Why did she walk all this way to draw water from here and then carry it all the way back into town?

Jesus hears someone coming and turns to see a Samaritan woman. She instantly recognizes Him as a Jew—perhaps by His clothes, or by the accent in His voice as He asks her:

> Will you give me a drink? (John 4:7 NIV)

The Samaritan woman seems taken aback that He would even speak to her, let alone ask her to give Him a drink. Therefore, she asks Him:

> *How is it that you, being a Jew, ask me for a drink, since I am a Samaritan woman?*

(The Jews have a well-known saying during this time: "Jews have no dealings with Samaritans." The Samaritan woman has heard it enough to quote it to Him.)

At a glance, Jesus sees her whole life. He knows everything about her. He knows her past failures and her present condition. The woman is alone. Not the loneliness you are thinking of—I mean really *alone*. She feels she is on a secluded island, even though she lives around others. Christ never talks around the edges of things. And so, He chooses to speak to the need in her life rather than answer her question directly. He goes right to the point of directing the conversation toward the spiritual issues rather than the physical—the soul rather than the body:

> *If you knew the gift of God, and who it is that says to you, "Give Me a drink," you would have asked Him, and He would have given you living water.*

Naturally enough, we see that she doesn't understand that He is speaking to her about who He is. And she responds by making two points and asking two questions:

- You have nothing to draw the water with.
- The well is deep.
- Where do you get this living water?
- Are you greater than Jacob, the one who dug this well?

Her response makes sense to one who is looking at the physical side of the account. Still Jesus responds to her in a way that remains consistent with the point He is making to her. He says:

> *Everyone who drinks of this water will thirst again, but whoever drinks of the water that I will give him will become in him a well of water springing up to eternal life.*

When she responds to Jesus' statement, she seems incapable of seeing the spiritual side of the conversation. Jesus knows that this woman doesn't know Him as the Messiah. She has never met Him before. Jesus' statements to her seem intended to get her to stop thinking about a drink of water and to realize who He is. She replies:

> *Sir, give me this water, so I will not be thirsty nor come all the way here to draw.*

It becomes clear that she doesn't understand the concept of "living water." This poor, uneducated Samaritaness seems bewildered at Christ's statements rather than grasping the spiritual side of what He is saying. She can see only the physical impossibility of never thirsting again. (In this respect she is not unlike Nicodemus, the educated rabbi of Jerusalem who had an earlier encounter with Christ. [7] However, Jesus doesn't rebuke the Samaritan woman as he did Nicodemus.)

Jesus steers the conversation toward her being a sinner (something she really understands) and her need for Him. He tells her to go and bring her husband back with her. She hesitates but answers honestly: "I have no husband."

> *Jesus said to her, "You have well said, 'I have no husband,' for you have had five husbands, and the one whom you now have is not your husband; this you have said truly."*

It is here I must clear up a misunderstanding, created by incorrect teaching, that has done this woman a terrible injustice.

So often, we have viewed this woman as promiscuous, moving from husband to husband until she is finished with the fifth and final one. By this time, we think, her morality had sunk so low that now she was living with a man she wasn't even married to.

This thinking is completely wrong. Let's look at my reasoning: The first-century woman was not permitted to divorce her husband. It was only the man who could divorce the woman, not the other way around. A wife was the property of her husband. For the pettiest of reasons (much like today), a man could dismiss his wife and send her packing. Therefore, the accurate way of viewing this Samaritaness is this: She has been married five times, but in each case, her husband found something unacceptable about her and rejected her.

Five times.

And the current man in her life doesn't have enough respect for her to give her a proper ceremony. This woman is not an immoral sinner whom Christ is rebuking, but rather a person who has been used, abused, and rejected by probably every man in her life. Christ recognizes this and does something with His immeasurable love that staggers me even to this moment.

Before I speak of it, first let us finish the account. We will return to what He does in a couple of pages.

The woman sees Him as godly because He can see her tattered past, and she takes this opportunity to ask a question that shows us her true heart. She asks, "Where should I go to worship, here at the mountain or in Jerusalem?" Jesus answers: "There is coming a time when God will be worshiped accurately, and it will not be on this mountain or in Jerusalem. The time is coming and is here now when God will be worshiped in people's spirits rather than in a specific place, and in truth in contrast to falsehoods." (My interpretation.)

Jesus gives her more hope than she has had in years by saying, "It is not where you worship, but how you worship." It is as if He pulls down a tether from Heaven and lovingly wraps it around her spirit.

The woman shows us her faith by saying:

> *"I know that Messiah is coming (He who is called Christ); when that One comes, He will declare all things to us." Jesus said to her, "I who speak to you am He."*

In other words, Jesus says to her, "The One you are waiting for is now speaking to you."

He speaks to her with the most profound and direct statement of self-revelation made in the New Testament. He says, "I am the Messiah, the savior of the world."

The woman is stunned.

Now as all this unfolds before us, the disciples are just returning. They are bewildered that He is conversing with this Samaritan woman. As they come up to

Christ, she leaves her water vessel and runs away, back into Sychar. Her mind is reeling from what has just taken place and the truths that she has been shown. Now she understands, and that spring of life is welling up inside of her in vaulting freedom. Casting aside the task of bringing water back into the village, she is now carrying inside her the *living water.*

Upon arriving in town, she begins to tell her story. A crowd gathers. She tries to catch her breath, and at the same time she relates what the man at the well told her:

> *Come, see a man who told me all the things that I have done; this is not the Christ, is it?*

After hearing the woman's story, the townspeople decide to go out and meet Jesus. While they're on their way, another conversation is taking place at Jacob's well.

Jesus seems to no longer be hungry. The disciples urge Him to eat the food they have just purchased in Sychar, but He refuses:

> *But He said to them, "I have food to eat that you do not know about."*

This statement by Christ makes them wonder whether someone else has brought Him something to eat while they were away. But, much like the Samaritaness, they don't understand that He is putting spiritual matters above physical comfort. And just as He did in the conversation with the woman, with loving patience He helps the disciples understand what is of the utmost relevance at the moment:

> *Jesus said to them, "My food is to do the will of Him who sent Me and to accomplish His work."*

The disciples don't understand this statement. They have left Judea for Galilee to do the very work He is speaking of, but now they are in Samaria. It will be at least another day before they arrive. They must be thinking, "We could never cause someone to believe in a place like this. These people are enemies of the Jews. There is no work to do here." To them it seems like the perfect time to eat.

The disciples hear, but don't understand, so Jesus uses an illustration. He looks out into the nearby fields. They have been wakened by the plow and the crops are growing. He says:

> *Do you not say, "There are yet four months, and then comes the harvest"? Behold, I say to you, lift up your eyes and look on the fields, that they are white for harvest.*

Jesus goes on speaking. Meanwhile, the woman is leading the townspeople to Him. Perhaps she comes into sight as He says, "Already he who reaps is receiving wages and is gathering fruit for life eternal."

Now we have a large gathering: the townspeople from Sychar, the disciples, the woman, Jesus Himself, and of course us. Another conversation begins, and what Jesus says to the people at the well causes them to no longer be enemies of these Jews. Instead, Jesus and the disciples are invited to come and stay in the town of Sychar. They stay two days in the town, and Jesus shares the Father's love with them and shows them who He really is. Many more believe because of what they hear Him say—not just because of the woman's testimony.

And it's all because of a discarded woman encountering the Messiah.

All because of a divine meeting on a hot dusty road in the middle of the day.

All because the Creator of heaven and earth wanted to show one of His children that He loved her in spite of what mankind thought.

Through whom did He choose to bring this message ? It was one woman whom Christ chose to be the spokesperson for His love to an entire people group.

Jesus had His first missionary:

- A woman the world thought little of.
- A woman who was not welcome even to draw water from the town she lived in.
- A woman who was forced to draw water when no one else was around.

- She was discarded by five men once they were finished with her. Moreover, her current lover didn't respect her enough to have a legal ceremony.

It's not too hard to realize how she felt about herself, is it? Still, in spite of it all, look at her words again:

> *I know that Messiah is coming (He who is called Christ); when He does He will declare all things to us.*

At that moment in time, Jesus chose to reveal who He was to her. This woman shared her experience and led the people to where Christ was. I said it in my last book and I'll say it again. Leonard Ravenhill said, "There are two kinds of Christians, those who point the way to the cross and those who lead the way to the cross."

To those who have been divorced—

To those who feel they have been discarded—

To those who are not welcomed in certain circles—

To those who have to go out of their way because of the prejudice of others—

To those who cannot get past that feeling of being stared at when they walk into a church—

Jesus says, "Look at me, don't look at them. *I who speak to you am He.*"

And just like the woman at the well, He chooses you.

You did not choose Him, but rather He chose you.

I have often wondered what this did for the woman's standing in the community. It seems quite obvious that the town no longer discriminated against her. This encounter with Jesus is the only thing that would have changed the town's perception of her. In addition, not only did it change their minds, but she was and will ever be known as the one through whom Christ chose to bring the living water.

Jesus didn't see a Samaritaness to be avoided. Jesus saw a hurt woman, and He listened not to her words as much as to what she was really saying. He spoke to the need in her life from the compassion in His heart. When most people offered her judgment, Jesus offered her understanding and forgiveness. Jesus gave her the love of God that reached across cultural and gender lines in a time and in a place when it was taboo in society to do so. Jesus crossed those lines by accurately showing us all how to treat a rejected woman. It is society and mankind that have created these boxes for others to live in, not Christ. Did you know that most mission organizations and denominations will not let a divorced person be a missionary? How sad and ironic for the cause of Christ, when He personally chose a five-time divorcée to be His first missionary to her people. And it may yet very well be the rejected woman whom Christ will use to lead us all to His person.

I can picture how the woman's life changed after this encounter. Now she catches her water from the well in town, but for the rest of her life she makes a pilgrimage, once a year or so, to the well where she first met Christ. She plays it all over in her head as she walks out to the fork in the road—every moment, every word, every expression. Maybe all the townspeople do, I don't know for sure. But one thing I do know: no one ever forgot what Christ did through her, and God has seen to that.

If you are hurting, I, Robert Scott Stiner, want you to know this: God loves you. Not the generic god that has been adopted by the world, but the personal God, the same God who sent His Son to Jacob's well outside of Sychar two thousand years ago. He is the same one who will go out of His way and wait for you to show up. He sees you right now, and He knows the burden you carry. Jesus still says to you today:

I who speak to you am He.

I don't know where you are in your life right now, but I do know this: Jesus is waiting by a well for you.

CHAPTER 15

Tears of Love

Luke 7:36–50

The woman is well known as a sinner. The Greek word in the text could be translated "prostitute," or it could mean something else. We see her standing on the perimeter of a crowd, intently listening to the words of Jesus.

Earlier in the day, it seems likely that Jesus spoke to the multitudes of the city as they gathered to hear the distinguished teacher. To some He is a prophet; to others He is the Savior, and to others He is nothing more than a sideshow. But we will focus our attention on the woman in the crowd, for this chapter is about her. It could be that she heard the message of Christ from someone else, and that caused her to act as she does. However, it appears to me that she heard firsthand the message of restoration that He gave. And what was that message? It is not recorded, and yet in substance it must have been identical to every message He would ever give: "Come unto Me, all you who labor and are heavy laden, and I will give you rest. Lean on Me . . . "

It is as if He is speaking only to her—speaking of the weight she carries and asking her to cast it upon His shoulders. She believes what He says, and she is changed.

The biblical story begins after the crowd has dispersed, and we pick up the account as Jesus accepts the invitation to the house of Simon, a Pharisee, for a meal. It is customary for the head of the Pharisees to invite itinerant rabbis over while they teach in their communities. But the woman in the crowd follows Jesus and discovers the home where He is dining.

The Pharisee has little respect for Christ. He does not offer Him the most common of courtesies, that of a foot bath upon entering one's home. It appears that Simon has invited Christ home more out of obligation than hospitality.

Because of the open architecture of Simon's house, the woman has access to the dinner party in an open courtyard or possibly an antechamber. She enters undetected, possibly because of the amount of guests. She brings with her a long-necked flask of perfume and enters the room where Christ is reclining. On bended knee, she bows before the One who has set her spirit free from the bondage of her past. She is overwhelmed by who He is and the gift that He has given her, and her tears fall like summer rain and wet the feet of Christ. She may not have intended for this to happen. With nothing else to wipe away her tears from His feet, she uses the only thing at her disposal—her long, flowing hair. Now she opens the vial of perfume and pours it over the feet of Christ. Instantly the room is overtaken with the beautiful fragrance.

And angels sing Heaven's own song of the heavy burden lifted as she bows to the One for whom her heart longs, in thanks for the words she never thought she would hear from her God: "Come unto Me."

The sinful woman has bowed before Christ, and He completely understands her tears of sorrow for the life she has lived. His compassion is turned toward the woman, who has offered Him the best that she could procure as well as a heavy burden—the very things He has asked of her. (No symbolism has ever been truer than what we see here: She represents the church, which has lost her way. But I shall save that for the study guide.)

Because of the scene the woman has made and the fragrance in the air, everyone's attention turns, obviously, toward the woman. Without saying a word, Simon the Pharisee thinks to himself:

> *If this man were a prophet, He would know who and what sort of person this woman is who is touching Him, that she is a sinner.*

Simon explains to himself the reason Jesus allowed this to happen. He thinks Christ does not know the woman. However, it is Simon who does not truly know her and Christ who does. Simon has the problem that many of us have—that of arranging people in classes. Jesus does not categorize people. And that statement alone can bring restoration to us all.

In the eyes of Christ, the woman is no less worthy than anyone else present in the home. Yet Simon fails to see this. The woman is exactly what he does not see. Simon chooses to see with conventional eyes rather than spiritual eyes, even though he is a religious leader.

May we not look through the eyes of convention in trying to turn this world on its ear.

Jesus has read Simon's unspoken thoughts. Now He shows him the accurate way of viewing the woman, but in a way that does not bring reproof to His host and thus disgrace him in front of his guests. The answer lies in the illustration given by Christ, which he knows Simon will understand. The illustration follows Simon's own reasoning, and he is forced to see the woman through new eyes.

By her own admission, the woman has known many sins, yet she is forgiven, as evidenced by the respect and honor with which Jesus treats her. Through Jesus' illustration, Simon sees that the woman's love is the result of much forgiveness.

What she has heard, what she believes to be God's true and faithful love—even to the most shipwrecked of lives—has now been opened to her. And Jesus turns to her and says:

Your faith has saved you; go in peace.

And it is the same for those who hear His message. He still speaks to you today. The messenger has changed, but it is still the same message, for it is His message. And He says to you, at this moment in your life:

Come unto Me, all you who are weary and heavy-laden, and I will give you rest. Take My yoke upon you and learn from Me, for I am gentle and humble in heart, and you will find rest for your souls. For My yoke is easy and My burden is light.

God loved us in that while we were yet sinners Christ died for us.

CHAPTER 16

Mary and Martha

Luke 10:38–42

It is in the autumn. Lazarus is a good man. He lives with his two sisters, Martha and Mary. The home is very nice and evidently belongs to Martha, although we know not how that came to be. But Lazarus is staying a few miles away in Jerusalem while the week-long festive celebration of the Feast of Booths[8] takes place. Martha is the mistress of the wealthy household, and indeed it is a busy time of year as the festivities are under way. She does have her younger sister Mary to share the chores and responsibilities.

Martha receives Christ into the home upon His arrival in Bethany. It seems Jesus has dismissed His disciples to go into the neighboring city of Jerusalem for the celebration. This is probably why He is alone in this account of the event. When Jesus sent out the seventy[9] as his forerunners, a couple of them might very well have stayed in Martha's home—hence her invitation for Jesus to stay there.

Now to the ladies of the story.

Like many older sisters, Martha has taken on a higher responsibility. At any time her brother could bring with him an honored and yet unexpected guest or two for lodging. If so, the woman of the house will have to hurriedly get the preparations and accommodations ready for the guests. Since Lazarus is presumably at the Feast of Booths, it is very likely he will arrive with guests from out of town to stay at the home. Someone has to handle the preparations. (As we know, they don't handle themselves.) This seems to be the type of person Martha is.

We will look at Mary in a moment.

Upon receiving Christ into their household, Mary and Martha are filled with excitement. They set about to honor Him as best they can. Martha, with her sense of responsibility, now wants to prepare a meal worthy of her guest. She hurries to and fro between the house and the courtyard, preparing the food. All the while, as she passes, she sees her sister Mary, rapt with attention at the feet of Christ, listening to His words. Martha can't do enough to show Him her hospitality. In trying to make all the dishes and get everything just right for the One she is honoring, she is literally distracted by the serving.

Mary too has found her way of honoring Jesus, but it is far different from Martha's. Her homage to Him is to forget all else and sit in the presence of Christ as He speaks words she has never heard before.

Time passes, perhaps quite a long time. All the while, Martha is busy preparing the food, and Mary is intently listening to the words of Christ. We can feel and understand the frustration in the voice of Martha as she says:

> *Lord, do You not care that my sister has left me to do all the serving alone? Tell her to help me.*

In the gentlest of tone, and with mild reproof—which appears in the repetition of her name—Jesus answers her:

> *Martha, Martha, you are worried and bothered about so many things; but only one thing is necessary, for Mary has chosen the good part, which shall not be taken away from her.*

It is not necessary to prepare so many dishes of food to honor Christ. Only one dish is needed for Him. And what Mary has chosen to do with her time is a good thing. Moreover, Christ is not going to take that away from her by having her prepare food as well. (My interpretation.)

Martha was busy preparing an elaborate meal to honor Christ, while Mary honored Him by being at His feet and allowing Him to minister to her. Martha truly was in service to Christ, but the service was not effective.

And we do the same thing in our lives at times.

Are you like me? I have found myself getting caught in the act of doing rather than the act of being. Sometimes we get so involved in the process that the process itself becomes the purpose, and we lose sight of Christ—even when we're doing things for Christ. But the "good part," as Jesus called it, is what we should be doing. Christ longs for us to sit at His feet in this life—to listen to what He has to say. He longs to teach us things that we have never fathomed about His love, but He cannot if we don't stop what we are doing and listen to Him.

It does not matter what you are doing for the sake of the cross if you do not first kneel at the foot of the cross.

CHAPTER 17

A Longtime Sickness

Luke 13:10–13

We know little about her, but what we do know speaks volumes. She was bound by Satan for eighteen years, to use the words of Jesus. Eighteen years bound, trapped, restricted, confined by Satan. We don't know the details, except that she is hunched over and cannot stand straight. That is a long time to suffer from a spirit of infirmity. And yet where do we find the woman? In the synagogue, in the house of worship. Can it be that this woman, racked with pain for all these years, has chosen not to let it stop her from worshiping God? Can it be that even the dark, clouded heart of the synagogue ruler, who believed that her suffering was a result of sin, can't keep her from worshiping her God? Let's you and me ask her the details of her circumstances when we get the chance in the next life. All I can tell you for sure is that she has suffered for eighteen years. If I suffer for eighteen minutes, I act like my world is coming to an end.

We are in the synagogue, and Jesus is teaching on this glorious Sabbath morning. And while the morning sun illuminates the earth for all to see, God's Son illuminates the fertile soil of the hearts of men and causes them to see spiritually—in contrast to the dark clouds of unbelief in the heart of the synagogue official who looks on.

Jesus sees the woman in the synagogue, and at that moment nothing else matters except her. The teaching stops. Jesus' compassion goes to the one who is suffering, and he calls her to come over to where He is. And as she hobbles her way through the crowd, we all watch. She looks at the ground as she works her way toward Christ, for she is hunched over in sickness from the spirit that torments her. Silence and expectancy fill the air as everyone watches. Here, I cannot speak for others, but I have no doubt that she believes in Christ, as evidenced by her obedience to His call to come and stand before Him.

With a sovereign command, Jesus says to her:

Woman, you are freed from your sickness.

He lays His hands on her, and her body straightens as straight as yours or mine. A gasp from the crowd immediately follows, and the woman begins glorifying God.

How long have you been with a sickness? And by the way, what type of sickness do you have? Is it crippling you to where you can't stand up straight? Has it caused you to take an unwanted seat in a chair that has wheels instead of legs? Maybe it is another type of sickness. It might be one of a spiritual nature—you know—the ones that are easily hidden from the world. They seem to be the type I am most susceptible to. They are the ones that cripple us and cause us not to stand up straight spiritually. And take it from me, if you are crippled spiritually, you are restricted from doing work in the Kingdom of God , just as you can't get out and weed the garden if you are physically crippled. There is also the sickness that makes me so mad that smoke almost comes out of my ears. It's the sickness of bad biblical teaching.

Whatever type of sickness you might be experiencing, remember the single most valuable lesson from this courageous and dear woman:

Remain faithful to God.

Even if He chooses not to deliver you from whatever ails you, remain faithful. That is exactly what this woman did. She must have known something that took me most of my life to figure out. She stayed faithful to her Lord

God by doing that which she knew to do, continuing her fellowship in spite of her condition. Our responsibility is to remain faithful and at the same time remember that the results have nothing to do with us—that's His department. So if we remain obedient to what we know to do according to His word, no matter how long it takes, He will be glorified through our faithfulness.

CHAPTER 18

Mary's Lasting Memorial

Matt. 26:6–13; Mark 14:3–9; John 12:1–8

It is six days until the Passover. Six days from now Christ will be suspended between Heaven and earth on the cross, to take away the sins that you and I commit. In six days history and future will see each other for the first time and know the reason for their creation. In six days Christ will walk a road, carry a cross, and ask His Father why—and all the while we will run and hide our faces. Yet it will have no bearing on His love for you and me. Why, you ask? Because

> *God demonstrates His own love toward us, in that while we were yet sinners, Christ died for us.*

It is six days before the Passover, and Jesus and His disciples reach Bethany, just outside Jerusalem. He is invited into a house that the Pharisees would not consider entering. It is the home of Simon the leper. Even though Simon doesn't have leprosy now, he still has retained the title. Jesus may very well have healed him earlier in one of His unrecorded miracles.

All are around the table, reclining as the evening meal is prepared for the special guest. Many of the townspeople have combined their resources to have this public meal and honor Him for all He has done for the people of Bethany. Martha and Mary are serving the food, and Lazarus, their brother, whom Christ raised from the dead, is seated at the table as well. Another woman named Mary arrives at the festive meal. She has with her a long, alabaster vial of extremely valuable, genuine spikenard.

Spikenard is aromatic anointing oil that is extracted from a plant that grows in East India. To give you an idea of the value of it, it would take the average worker one year's wages to buy it. In other terms, only two-thirds of the cost would be enough money to feed five thousand men and their families a meal.[10]

Who is this woman Mary? We no nothing else of her, but there are questions we can ask:

- Does she know Jesus?
- Did He heal her of something?
- Did Jesus tell her as well of His impending death?

- Does she believe what the disciples had a hard time believing—that His death was near?
- Is that why she anoints Him, for His burial?

It certainly seems that it could be the case.

What does she do for sure ? She assumes a position that is the obligation of the servants in Simon's household: She bows and anoints the feet of Christ with spikenard—the best thing she can offer Him. It is costly. It is valuable. And it is worthy of His burial. She anoints His head with it, and the home where Christ is dining is filled with a sweet aroma. In parallel, when we bow at His feet today, He enters our home and the sweet aroma of His grace fills every space.

Judas's view is distorted because he is a thief; he can't see past the financial side of the situation, and he calls it a waste. But what Judas calls a waste, Jesus calls a lasting memorial.

Whatever you have, honor Christ with it. With the best of whatever you have, anoint the feet and head of Christ.

Do you have time?
Do you have ability?
Do you have a home to open up?
Do you have a listening ear for a co-worker?
Do you have breath still in you?
With what you possess, honor Christ.

It will be a lasting memorial to Him that will affect everyone around you. Don't worry about the inevitable complaints the world will throw at you. Just stay at the feet of Christ in servanthood, and you will never be safer, you will never be more protected, and you will never be more loved.

No, we don't know much about this Mary, but we know she is the one who anointed the Savior of the world for His burial. It was Jesus who said that the memory of her action would live forever.

In a world of Marthas, be the next Mary!

CHAPTER 19

Mary Magdalene

Note to Mary

Mary, where is your past? Where is the information I need to bring you to life again and show women how they can relate to you? How can I get inside of your heart and see your wounds and the restoration that Christ gave you?

I know—I'll think about you and write what I do know and feel. And on that fateful day, you can straighten what I have bent. I'm fairly confident that I will get it right, but I am completely confident that our Holy Spirit will use this chapter in a way that will help the cause of Christ.

Her name is Mary Magdalene. She has no last name, so we call her Mary of the town of Magdala (Mary Magdalene). The town she lives in is nestled on the shore of the Sea of Galilee and is one of the wealthiest in the land, due to the dye-making in the region. Other than this we know nothing of her residence or her stature in her community. We know that Christ healed her by casting seven demons out of her, but we do not know what caused them or even the circumstances around her pain. All we see are the edges of what Christ has done for her and the result of His compassion. From the few blurred snapshots of her life that we have to investigate, one thing is for sure: she is faithful to Christ. She is faithful in her support of Him and faithful in following Him.

My account of the life of Mary Magdalene is my own rendering. That is to say in plainer words, it is fiction. Most everything you read is biblical; however, even though the four gospels all mention Mary, they do not line up with one another in a way that would be conducive to writing about her in story form. If you read the biblical accounts, you will see that I have attempted to say what I feel takes place in certain situations. This paragraph is my disclaimer, so put down those stones.

I want to start at the end of what we know about her. Two major points, really.

First, she is faithful.

The disciples have fled for their lives against the backdrop of Roman brutality. And now Christ is suspended between heaven and earth, flanked by thieves and in excruciating pain, as His life slowly, methodically slips away. He looks up through the blood and tears and through the pain to see that most all of His followers have abandoned Him. His head dips down again as He labors for His next breath. Somewhere between the few statements He makes on that instrument of torture, His head rises again and He sees, off in the distance, a small band of women, watching, weeping. He can see James and John's mother, and Zebedee's wife and some others, and then He spots her. (I believe that at this moment, through the pain, He smiles—at least in His heart, if not outwardly). In the midst of that band of women stands Mary Magdalene, whom He has delivered from terrible bondage to seven demons. She has followed Him after He healed her; she followed Him from Galilee and she has now followed Him to the cross. She has followed Him to what she thinks is the end. And Christ says, "You are the one. You are the one whom I have chosen to be the first. I will prove that *I Am*[11] to you first!"

It's Sunday, early morning, long before the sun comes up. It's the greatest morning eternity can ever know. It has been a worthless attempt to try to rest, so Mary rises and meets the other women. Upon their meeting they break down in tears again. And although it takes a while, they gain their composure and resolve to do the task that lies before them. So, with oils and spices of considerable weight in hand, they start down the path toward the tomb.

And all the while God, Jesus, all of Heaven, and now you and I are watching. They are going to the tomb to prepare Christ's body for burial, even though they are not sure if they can do it once they get a close look at Him.

The Roman soldiers have beaten Him and shredded His back until there is no skin left. His face is almost unrecognizable because of the swelling where they pulled sections of His beard and hair out.

The women walk in silence down the path, carrying the necessary provisions, knowing nothing of the latest events that have occurred. All they know is that while Christ was alive, He changed their lives forever. He restored them in a far deeper way than they could have ever imagined. They vowed to follow Him; to support His ministry, which would do for others what He had done for them; and to serve Him.

Now it is all over for the women. Still, with this last homage to Him, they come to prepare His body and say their final farewell—to serve Him one last time. But Christ is not quite finished with the occupancy of His body, although Mary Magdalene and the other women know nothing of it. The spices Mary is bringing will not be used this day nor any other day on the body of her Savior.

A few minutes before the sunrise, when the hue of light begins to appear in the eastern sky, the ground is rocked by a violent earthquake. It finally passes, and the women steady themselves and continue the now short distance to the tomb. Mary Magdalene hastens a few steps ahead of the others and is the first to arrive. Fear grips her as she stares at what she sees. Two guards lie on the ground as if they have been killed. The huge stone that blocked the entrance of the tomb is now rolled away from it, and a huge angel is sitting on the stone as if it were no more than a small piece of furniture to him. The other women arrive, and they too freeze in fear.

> *The angel said to the women, "Do not be afraid; for I know that you are looking for Jesus who has been crucified. He is not here; He has risen, just as He said. Come, see the place where He was lying." (Matt. 27:5–6)*

Mary Magdalene slowly walks toward the opening, and the others follow close behind her. Their spices and oils now lie discarded and leaking on the ground. They never take their eyes off the angel as they slowly pass. They step over the guards, who now look much like their spices, and enter the tomb.

Another angel sits near the head of the garment that held Christ—still wrapped, but flat like an empty cocoon. The other angel enters and stays near the foot of the garment.

After the women have seen for themselves, they are still frightened, but become ecstatic at the same time. One begins to shout with joy, another tries to keep from hyperventilating, and still another falls on her knees and says, "Hosanna, Hosanna to the King," over and over again. Mary Magdalene remembers Jesus' words. Standing speechless, she stares at the angelic beings as if for some type of guidance. The angel begins to speak, and the group quiets to listen. The angel says:

> *Go quickly and tell His disciples that He has risen from the dead (make sure you tell Peter); and behold, He is going ahead of you into Galilee, there you will see Him; behold, I have told you.*

The women slowly back away from the tomb and the angels, then take off running down the path. Filled with fear and great joy, hands full of the bottoms of their dresses so they can run faster, they carry with them the news that all of Christianity hinges on:

Christ is risen from the dead!

Mary Magdalene takes a shorter route, down another fork in the path. As she runs, she sees a man up ahead of her.

And Mary Magdalene becomes the first person to see Christ after His resurrection. She is the one to whom Christ gives the honor, and her lips will first utter the words to Peter: "He has risen, just as He told us He would!"

My second major point about the life of Mary Magdalene is that she is never forgotten.

Never forgotten means always remembered. And that is what you are to Christ. He has not forgotten nor will He ever forget your name, lose track of you, or lose sight of you. Your wanderings may very well take you far from

Christ if that is what you choose, and yet He will always be your next breath. If you are worried about your future failures, convinced that you can't get away from that which holds you, then remember this.

Jesus was once wrapped in a manger, but that manger could not hold Him long. Now He was wrapped in a tomb, and it could not hold Him for long as well. And because of that one act, whatever you think is holding you down will not hold you forever. And about your future sins: remember that all your sins were in the future when compared to the cross. From God's perspective, everything you would do would be in the future, compared to the time that His Son died for you. No freer words have ever been proclaimed than these, **because He lives, I can face tomorrow.**

Conclusion

In this book, I started out once again to tell the story of people whom Christ had changed. But once again He told the story of my life through theirs, and I was changed. In the Scriptures, every person who encounters Christ is changed, and the stories of those encounters have the power to change all of us, including me. I just was unable to see it at times. I can hardly believe what I have seen for the first time through these ancient stories. It seems they have changed me again, and I am a little farther along than I was yesterday with our Savior and Lord.

We are now 2,000 years removed from the time that Christ walked this earth as God and man. And the shadow of His cross is still cast over this earth. That cross, the emblem of enduring spiritual freedom, was made from a tree—but before that tree was cut down, it shed seeds that could give life to countless other trees. Perhaps its offspring cover the land now. The scriptural accounts that I have written about have done the same—Christ's encounters with people, the effect He had on them, and the restoration that He wrought have multiplied in my life and in countless others.

I'm tremendously honored to write a book that you would read, and in no way do I take it lightly. But at times while writing it, I felt as though it were a marvelous gift of intimacy that God was giving to me alone. That is what God does in our lives: He draws us near to Him and intimately explains to us the gospel mysteries, like a father teaching his child. Let us, therefore, draw near to Him, allowing His grace to purify our lives so that we might obey Him in the fullness of His strength.

Chapter 1

1. Why would it have been so hard for Jairus to come to Christ for anything?
2. At this time in history, there was a certain stigma unfairly put on people like this bleeding woman. Discuss unfair stigmas put on people today.
3. Do you feel this woman had great faith or the smallest amount of faith? Explain your answer.
4. What status do you believe the woman possessed in her community after Christ restored her?
5. How can the answers to these first four questions apply to our lives today?

Chapter 2

1. Why did Jesus give this response to His mother upon her initial statement? Then, why did Mary continue to instruct the servants to do whatever Jesus said?
2. What did Jesus mean when He said that His hour had not yet come?
3. Discuss all the different ways Jesus kept this wedding from an embarrassing disaster. Who were the people He helped by the miracle?
4. Who do you think was the first to know of what Jesus did?
5. What do you think I meant when I said, "To know about Jesus is water but to know Jesus is wine"?

Chapter 3

1. There were different types of people around Jesus, watching how He would respond to the needs of the nobleman begging for His help. Describe what you believe those types of people were.
2. Do they still exist as you share the gospel? Explain.
3. Should your responses to these groups vary ? If so, how?
4. Discuss the type of faith that you believe the nobleman had.
5. Did it change?

Chapter 4

1. How can sin trap a person spiritually?
2. How can it paralyze someone?
3. How can a person get used to living in despair?
4. The people around the Pool Bethesda put their faith in something that had no help at all in it. Have you ever put your faith in something or someone that has let you down? If so, think of the process that got you to that point and the process that brought you back to the restoration of God.
5. Why did Jesus go to the Pool?
6. Why does Jesus still ask us today if we wish to get well, even though we are believers?
7. Our pallet is our testimony of what Christ has brought us through. What is your pallet?

Chapter 5

1. Normally it is in retrospect that we see the hand of God. Explain a time in your life when you saw the hand of God once you were on the other side of the encounter.
2. In this account of the life of Jesus, we see that Jesus used Peter's boat as a pulpit. Share some ways that God has used you to share the love of God in an unorthodox way.
3. When Jesus teaches us, it is always in terms we can understand. If not, then it wouldn't be teaching at all. Think of some of the ways that our Lord has taught you to see a deeper understanding of Himself.
4. Christ was after Peter's obedience, not a complete understanding of the situation. Does He ask the same of us today? If so, explain.

Chapter 6

1. Do you think there are demon-possessed people today?
2. If so, what forms do you think they take?
3. How do you think the enemy of the cross has changed his strategy from the time of Christ till now?
4. What would have gone though your mind if you witnessed this firsthand?

Chapter 7

1. Leonard Ravenhill once told me, "God doesn't hear prayers, He hears desperate prayers." What lessons can we learn about bringing a desperate need to Christ?
2. How did Peter's mother-in-law respond when Christ healed her? What does that response teach us about how to respond to what He has done for us?
3. What did this healing do for Peter?
4. What did this healing do for Peter's mother-in-law?
5. What did it do for Peter's wife?

Chapter 8

1. Describe all the players in this account. What were their views about Jesus before and after the healing?
2. What has this chapter shown us about our faith in what Christ can do for others?
3. Why does Jesus still tell us today, after we have been healed, to do three specific things: 1) Rise; 2) Pick up your pallet; and 3) Go home?

Chapter 9

1. Why is it that more often than not, God chooses to use those who have been broken on the wheels of living to reach out to certain types of people?
2. Elaborate on this phrase: "It is not our wounds that give us our identity, but rather our scars."

Chapter 10

1. What makes us believe that because we have sinned we cannot approach God?
2. How does God respond when we know what is right and yet choose to do what is wrong? Romans 7–8 has part of the answer.
3. The elders told Jesus that the centurion was worthy. But they failed to realize that what made him worthy was the belief that he wasn't. Explain this in different terms. How does this concept apply to our lives today?

Chapter 11

1. This chapter is about many things, but I would like to focus on one particular aspect of it: death and life. Discuss ways that you have died and the way that Christ has brought you back to life.
2. How does death affect the people around it?
3. What are the types of death that bring life?

Chapter 12

1. At the beginning of this account in John, we find Jesus beginning His day with prayer. I find that my best writing comes from the first waking of a new day. Why does this concept of beginning the day in fellowship with God seem to be so important?
2. We all stand guilty before God. How is it that Christ gives us a way out of paying the price that we should have to pay?
3. What other responses could Christ have given to the Pharisees?
4. In this chapter I have alluded to things that I believe happen in heaven that we are not aware of. What things do we know for sure happen in heaven as a reaction to events here on earth, as written in the Bible?
5. Why didn't Christ judge the woman guilty?

Chapter 13

1. The Syrophoenician-Greek woman's petition was not even acknowledged the first time she cried out to Jesus. Why do you think that is, and what does it teach us about our own prayer lives?
2. The woman's prayer seemed to be answered when it became the root of her need. What does this tell us about prayer?

Chapter 14

1. Why did Jesus not go with the disciples to get the food?
2. Because Jesus knew everything about this woman, He was able to speak to the need in her life, rather than address the questions she was asking, by guiding the conversation to Himself. How does He do this in our lives today?
3. Why did the Samaritaness say that Jews have no dealing with the Samaritans?
4. What do I mean when I say that Christ never talks around the edges of things?
5. This woman is without a doubt the first recorded missionary for Christ. Why, then, do you feel that some denominations don't allow divorced people to be missionaries?
6. What type of faith did the Samaritaness have in Christ before and after the encounter?

Chapter 15

1. I believe that the woman could have felt that Jesus was speaking only to her if she were indeed in the crowd. Has there been a time when you were in a crowd, but you felt as if God was speaking directly to you ? If so, share your experience.
2. How do we as believers arrange people in classes?
3. What needs to happen in our lives before we can stop this practice?
4. In this account, Jesus makes the perfect statement for the situation He is in. What is required for us to make that kind of statement in situations we find ourselves in?

Chapter 16

1. I find myself being a Martha type more than a Mary type most of the time. The feeling of having to do something for Christ instead of just resting in Christ is more often than not in the forefront of my mind. "If I don't do it, it's not going to get done," I say to myself. Explain the differences between Martha and Mary and what can we learn from both of them.

Chapter 17

1. Sometimes suffering is caused by outside forces that we have no control over. And yet people can cause you to think that you have done something wrong. It is important to remember that Christ never condemns you.
2. How did this woman remain faithful to what she felt she should do all those years?
3. What does it speak of to our lives in Christ?
4. The results of what God chooses to do are up to Him. What is our responsibility?

Chapter 18

1. Why is it that our actions have no bearing on God's love for us?
2. What is some of the symbolism of this anointing of Jesus?
3. Through this woman, how and what have we learned to give to Christ?
4. Explain in your own words what my last statement in the chapter means.

Chapter 19

1. How did this woman follow Christ? There are several ways.
2. How is it that Mary Magdalene is never forgotten?
3. How is it that you are never forgotten?
   Read *Lessons from a Venetian Vinedresser*

[1] This account of healing by touching Jesus' clothes also occurs in
[2] Jesus was a Jew and born in a region of the world where men and women had olive skin, dark hair, and dark eyes.
[3] It is my belief that the stirring of the waters was an underground thermal spring.
[4] When evening came, the witnesses to the morning's miracle in the synagogue brought everyone who was sick to Peter's home, and Christ healed them all. Thus, we have an account of a morning, midday, and evening in the life of Christ.
[5] Some teach that Jesus gave harsh answers to this woman because she was a heathen. They are wrong—not bad, just wrong. Jesus never has and never will react harshly to someone who cries out to Him no matter whom the person.
7

[6] The term means "little dogs," or "house dogs."
[8] The Feast of Booths, also known as the Feast of Tabernacles, commemorated Israel's wilderness experience.
[9] See Luke 10:1.
[10] See Mark 6:37.
[11] See Exodus 3:13–14, John 8:58.

Other Books by Robert Scott Stiner

Lessons from a Venetian Vinedresser

Available from your local bookstore or online at www.amazon.com

To comment on this book, or any other books by Robert, or to schedule the author for a speaking engagement, please visit:

www.robertscottstiner.com

To order additional copies of

Encountering Christ

Have your credit card ready and call
Toll free: (877) 421–READ (7323)
or send $14.99* each plus $5.95 S&H** to

Pleasant Word, A Division of WinePress Publishing
PO Box 428
Enumclaw, WA 98022

or order online at: www.pleasantword.com

*WA residents, add 8.4% sales tax
**add $2.00 S&H for each additional book ordered

All orders are insured & shipped via UPS Ground

Printed in the United States
46947LVS00007B/154

9 781579 215484